BOEING TRIVIA

CARL M. CLEVELAND

CMC Books

Seattle, Washington

Copyright © 1989 by Carl M. Cleveland

Published by CMC Books
                1101 Seneca Street #1201
                Seattle, Washington 98101

Second Printing

ISBN 0-9622194-0-1
Library of Congress Catalog Card Number: 89-90966

Cover design by Phyllis Wood
Photos courtesy Boeing Historical Archives
Typesetting and production by Anne and Merle Dowd

Do you have a favorite story or incident for inclusion in a possible BOEING TRIVIA II book? If so, please send it to the author at CMC Books. See address above.

Contents

7. Engineering   69
Even austere slip-stick artists provide breaks in the day's routine

8. Plant Protection—Company CIA   80
The unique Stan Leith and his minions

9. Manufacturing   97
Doxies "assist" war effort

10. The Military   108
Which sometimes took its job—and itself—too seriously

11. La Femme   136
Nylons, romances and caramels

12. Public Relations   145
A gorgeous nude and a million golf balls

13. Flight Test   159
Slim and Tex—two who shook up management

14. New York - Washington   173
The "Tuesday Musical"—unique public relations group

15. Public Relations Types   182
Zany romantics, somehow they got the job done

16. Potpourri   188
Kids, red Indians and friendly lions

Index   209

Acknowledgments

It is customary for authors to mention and thank those who have been of particular assistance in the various stages of producing a book. To thank everyone who contributed to this work would require pages. However, a few persons gave extra of their time and expertise. Among them:

T Wilson, Vern Manion, Dean Thornton, Jim Boynton, Tex Johnston, David Olson, Paul Spitzer, Marilyn Phipps, Bob Lamson, Dick Rouzie, Al Heiland, Barbara Loar, Stan Little, Karl Martinez, Dora Hunter, Kay Kelley, Keith Kinsman, Fred Baker, Harold Olsen, Clancy Wilde, Ken Luplow, Mark Nevils, Chuck O'Brien, Elmer Vogel, Ben Wheat and Dave Peterson.

Extensive material has been extracted from taped interviews with Bill Allen, made shortly after he withdrew from active participation in directing the company.

Especial thanks to Phyllis Wood for cover design and valuable suggestions regarding format. And to Merle and Anne Dowd for preparation of copy for printing, handling all details of printing and overall supervision of the project, as well as guidance for a tyro publisher.

For Mariah Kari

Who cannot yet read and will
therefore accept this book without
comment or criticism

Introduction

The Boeing Company a monolithic entity; a cold, impersonal giant? Wrong! Boeing is not a set of incorporation papers filed in Delaware. Official papers produce nothing, accomplish no ends. Boeing is people. And Boeing was, and is, but a microcosm of the communities in which it operates. It is made up of sharp managers, outstanding engineers, scientists of great achievement, skilled workers and expert technicians, secretaries, artists, editors. All with the ambitions, the frustrations, the challenges of everyday living. Individually, as in any large community, you will find those of highest rectitude, and, yes, a few, a very few, con artists and ne'er-do-wells, a bit of thievery, minor rule breaking, intrigues and arranged seductions.

Pervading, however, was, and is, the serious task of running a huge company, turning out its incomparable products, planning for the future. Yet in this strict attention to business, unusual occurrences, bizarre events, unique characters and humorous incidents surface here and there, serving to confirm that Boeing people are no different than others. And they demonstrate that grimness is not necessarily a prerequisite for operation of a large and successful company.

Yes, Boeing has its many facets. It is the purpose of this book to show that people at Boeing can laugh and experience the ridiculous and the unusual without any loss of efficiency.

You will find no plot in the succeeding pages, nor any chronology in the reporting. Rather what follows is a series of vignettes loosely joined, yet each an entity in itself. While scores of persons are named, titles of the individuals are not indicated unless germane to the incident being related. This elimination of titles is necessary because the time-span of the book is that of the company itself. In that period people progressed through various work classifications with attendant changes of title. For example, in his steps upward from hired-in rookie engineer to chairman and chief executive of the company, T Wilson carried many different titles. To repeat them each time his name appears would be confusing and redundant.

An index of given names and proper nouns will be found at the back of the book.

Scores of persons, both in and outside Boeing, were interviewed in the course of gathering the material for this work. I can attest to the factuality of those incidents in which I had a part. As to other material I have full faith in the integrity and recall of those whom I interviewed.

The author recognizes that he has only highlighted the amusing and unusual as have occurred at

Boeing over the years. Each employee will have his own "I remember when . . ." to add to the collection. Actually the entire book is an acknowledgment to all those who "remember the time . . ."

Abbreviations and references used throughout the book.

AIA—Aerospace Industries Association
IATA—International Air Transport Association
Ad Bldg.—Administration or headquarters building on East Marginal Way
DPC Bldg.—Defense Production Corporation building erected by the government at Plant Two during World War II
DPC Annex—Secondary to the main DPC building
P.R.—Public Relations Department
The Press or Media—Newspapers, magazines, radio and TV
East Marginal Way—Principal street on which Ad Bldg. and Plant Two front
WWII—World War II
TWA—Trans-World Airways

1

Headquarters

Fountain of wisdom—salted by an occasional character and bits of humor

Modest to Lush—From the late '30s when it was completed to the mid-'70s, the Boeing Administration Building, on Seattle's East Marginal Way and just across the street from Boeing Field, was modest in decor and furnishing. It reflected the tight ship administered by Phil Johnson and later Bill Allen, the two presidents of the era.

In keeping with great expansion of its business and the multiplicity of its customers, headquarters today reflects the ambiance of "Big Business." Deep-piled rugs, soft divans and impressive conference tables are the norm. Art and sculpture lend a note of elegance to walls and hallways.

Whether spartan or lush, headquarters over the

years has spiced routine business with its quota of humor, surprises and interesting characters.

✈ ✈ ✈ ✈ ✈

Rough Landing—Typical of such characters was Fred Collins, Boeing sales manager in the 1940s. Son of a prominent Seattle family, debonair, gregarious, Fred had been an airmail pilot and a flight instructor before joining Boeing. He was one of those men whom fate or the unusual seems to pursue relentlessly. In his earlier flying days he came in for a landing on Boeing Field in a P-12. His brakes locked and the plane flipped upside down. Fred was hanging there by his seat belt when he unthinkingly unfastened it. Pow! Onto his head on the runway.

In the days before traffic signals or stop signs, Fred was waiting impatiently in his car at Boren Avenue wanting to cross busy Olive Way. Cars came in both directions, never far enough apart for Fred to cross. Finally he saw two cars coming down Olive Way with he judged enough space between them for him to get through. He gunned his engine and shot forward just as the first car passed, only to discover that it was towing the following car with a long chain. The three cars spun down the street in wide circles until they finally came to a stop and could be untangled.

On another occasion Fred happened to be driving in the far reaches of Ballard, an area of the city he and his wife rarely visited. At a blind corner Fred collided broadside with a car coming from his right. The irate driver stepped out. It was Mrs. Collins.

Fred was both witty and blunt. Boeing had arranged a cocktail party in a famed Washington, DC, hotel for one of its foreign customers. At the same time, in a larger adjoining room, President Roosevelt was the principal luncheon speaker and Dunninger, the mind reader, was to provide entertainment.

As Fred stood chatting with a guest, Dunninger came up. "Say, fellows," he said sotto voce, "can you tell me where the men's room is?"

Fred looked at him. "For crying out loud! You can read minds and you can't tell where the men's room is?"

✈ ✈ ✈ ✈ ✈

Howard on the Phone—Howard Hughes, eccentric millionaire, was without doubt the most difficult customer Boeing ever had to deal with. He carried on most of his business by telephone and at night. Further, his calls were long-winded.

"I never talked to him face to face, and he bought about 300 million dollars' worth of airplanes from us," Bill Allen recalled. "I remember one night in particular. I was out in the yard, and Mrs. Allen called that Mr. Hughes was on the line. I went into the library and stretched out on the davenport because I knew it would be a long-winded call and took up the phone. That was at 9:05 p.m. It wasn't a conversation, it was a Hughes monologue—and it terminated at 1:30 in the morning.

"One of the men Hughes put in as president of TWA was Carter Burgess," Allen recalled on another occasion. "I called Carter and asked him if he knew that we were building some expensive planes for his company, and no one from TWA had been to see them.

"I invited him and Bob Rummel to come to Seattle and out to the house for dinner. Just as they drove in, I got a phone call from Hughes. I told him his new president of TWA had just arrived and I would have to saw it off. Hughes asked, 'What kind of looking fellow is he? You know, I've never seen him.'

"I went downstairs and apologized to Carter for the delay. I said I've just been talking to your boss. Burgess said, 'Is that so. What kind of guy is he?'"

✈ ✈ ✈ ✈ ✈

Give Them to Charity—The company has a policy forbidding any individual from accepting gifts from a supplier, customer, media person, or any person or firm with which the company does business. It was painful and sometimes hard to explain the return of innocuous gifts. Nevertheless, rules are rules.

One day a package was delivered to Bill Allen's office. It contained a beautiful custom-made fly rod from Abercrombie and Fitch's New York store. With it was a gift card from C.R. Smith, president of American Air Lines. Bill promptly returned the gift to C.R. with an explanation of company policy.

A couple of weeks later the same package returned. This time it was addressed to Miss Nancy Allen, care of Bill Allen, Boeing. An enclosed note from C.R. explained that he was sending the rod to Nancy and that he was damn sure company rules didn't apply to Bill's daughter. C.R.'s notes were always written in longhand and without the use of capital letters.

I found myself in a quandary one Christmas. I received in the mail a beautiful set of cuff links from Dr. Hyman, publisher of *Interavia* in Geneva, Switzerland. The publication is world famous. I went to Allen and said, "I know the rule on gifts, but there is no way I can explain to Dr. Hyman the return of these cuff links. He just wouldn't understand. I'm afraid he would be insulted."

Bill pondered for a moment and said, "Well, all

right, give them to some charity." I had always been an exponent of charity beginning at home. I still have the cuff links and the tiny watch encased in one of them still keeps perfect time.

✈ ✈ ✈ ✈ ✈

Allen Shoots Manion—Bill Allen was one of the first to purchase a revolutionary Land camera which took, developed and produced a finished picture in less than a minute.

For several years Allen had been presenting 25-year pins to veteran employees. Such presentations took place in his office. So that the employee would have visual evidence of his honor, pictures were taken of the presentations.

Vern Manion was the photographer usually assigned to take these pictures. In striving for the best poses, he had no qualms in ordering Allen to "Pull down your coat, please; adjust your tie; look over to the left; now give him a handshake."

Shortly after buying his Land camera, Allen summoned Manion to his office.

When Manion walked in, Allen said, "Vern, you've been ordering me around for years, now it's my turn. Sit down over there. Pull your sweater down. Don't look at the camera. Sit up straight. Smile!"

The session went on, Allen giving Manion each picture as taken. "Okay, boss," Manion finally said, "I give up!"

✈ ✈ ✈ ✈ ✈

Never Under-Estimate the Power—The Allens were driving in from the airport one day. Passing the main Boeing plant, Mrs. Allen observed, "Bill, that headquarters building of your looks awfully shabby. Some of the paint is peeling."

A week later the building was resplendent in its new coat of paint.

✈ ✈ ✈ ✈ ✈

T's New Office—When T Wilson took over Bill Allen's duties as president of Boeing, Allen retained the title of chairman and kept his third floor office. It was deemed proper that the new president have an office in keeping with the title and responsibilities. An office in the northeast corner of the building was remodeled, refurnished and a bathroom, complete with shower and accoutrements, installed. T was quite naturally proud of his new office.

Enter an opportunistic group of plotters, including Tex Bouillioun, Tom Reidinger and Ben Wheat. With plans completed, they awaited the right occasion, which occurred when T called a meeting in his office.

The session had barely started when Wilson was summoned to Allen's office. With his departure, the plotters activated their scheme. The conference in Allen's office lasted only a few minutes. As it ended, Allen said, "By the way, T, I haven't seen your new setup. How do you like it?"

"Come on right now and I'll show you," Wilson replied eagerly. Arriving at the other end of the hall, T said, "First I want to show you my new bathroom." He swung back the door to be greeted by a sweet feminine voice, "Oh, hi, T sweetie!" To his consternation a good-looking young lady, clad in a bath towel wrapped tightly around her well-designed body, stepped from his shower. T tried to back out of the room, but Allen effectively blocked his way.

At the assembled group's roar of laughter, it dawned on T that he was the victim of a plot in which Allen played a key role.

✈ ✈ ✈ ✈ ✈

Stan's Plan—T Wilson had the unenviable task of directing the tightening of the labor force and effecting cost reductions in the crisis which faced Boeing in 1970. That he achieved the goals and helped bring the company through that lean period is, no doubt, one of the reasons Wilson was tapped to succeed Bill Allen as president and, later, chairman of the company.

"Stan Leith, plant protection manager, was the best manager in the company in regard to meeting budgets," Wilson says. "But he was also the toughest in the company to negotiate with.

"In that period of marked reduction in costs, I had ruled that overhead must come down in the same proportion as direct costs. One of the steps we were taking to reduce costs was to dispose of old Plant One, the first Boeing production plant, located on the Duwamish River. The place was a pile of junk; there was only one decent building on the property.

"Leith gave me a strong argument against reduction in his guard and fireman personnel. 'I'll go along with your program if you insist,' he said. 'But I want to go on record that if there is any more reduction in the number of guards and firemen at Plant One, the place will burn down.'

"I made the casual statement that if the place did burn, it wouldn't be catastrophic. Immediately Leith said, 'Look, we've got three or four known arsonists working in the plant here. We keep a close eye on them. If you'll get a couple of them assigned over there at Plant One, the place won't last a week!'

"I said, 'Stan, I've got troubles enough already. That kind of help I don't need.'"

✈ ✈ ✈ ✈ ✈

Varied Visitors—Visitors to Boeing have run the full gamut from royalty to school children. Escorting some of these visitors was both pleasurable and an education.

Arthur Fiedler, popular conductor of the Boston Pops orchestra for a number of years, was a most delightful person. White hair, trim mustache, erect carriage and a gentlemanly manner were his trademarks.

After a brief stop at Bill Allen's office, I drove the maestro to Renton where the C-97 was being built. I took him up into the cockpit of a finished airplane. He astonished our technical people with his knowledge of the instruments on the panel, their function, and the intelligent questions he asked.

To me, Arthur Godfrey, ukelele strumming radio star of the '50s, was a bit of an egoist. With a Boeing car and driver, I picked him up at the Olympic Hotel. On the way to Renton. I suggested to the driver that we go by way of the Mercer Island floating bridge. As we crossed Lake Washington, Mt. Rainier loomed crystal-clear to the south. It looked almost as though the mountain were at the very end of the lake.

"Mt. Rainier is 60 miles away," I explained. "If you will look in the opposite direction, to the left, you will see Mt. Baker, 80 miles distant."

As I continued to extol the beauties of the lake and mountains, Godfrey interrupted, "Hey, you got a radio in this car? My program should be on and I wanna hear it."

Godfrey was a pilot in his own right, even if he did

get into a bit of a jam for buzzing a control tower in his DC-3. He and Tex Johnston got on well, and later they joined on a tiger hunt in India. Tex bagged a beautiful cat whose pelt adorns a wall of his home.

Before he became Shah of Iran, Prince Pahliv was a visitor to Plant Two. He too was knowledgeable about aviation. He later was exiled and spent his last days as a man without a country, rejected by Egypt and Mexico before Jimmy Carter gave him temporary haven in the U.S.

Henry Luce, co-founder and president of Time, Inc., was as old-hat as your next door neighbor. After he had toured the plant and had a session with Bill Allen, I was delegated to return him to his hotel.

At the Olympic he said, "Come on in. Let's have a drink."

I envisioned full bragging rights. I would casually say, "Yesterday I had a scotch and soda with Henry Luce."

At the bar he said, "I'll have a Coca Cola with a slice of lime." Then he asked what I could like.

"Make mine a coke too, but no lime please."

We westerners take our drinks straight.

✈ ✈ ✈ ✈ ✈

It Wouldn't Dare!—Earthquakes are rare, but not entirely unknown in Seattle. One of the most severe, doing major damage throughout the city, hit at 11:58 a.m. on April 18, 1949.

The Boeing cafeteria, seating some 1500 people, was filled when the first shocks rocked the building. Overhead light fixtures swayed wildly. Stacked dishes on the serving counters crashed and windows shattered.

A mad rush from the cafeteria and various buildings ensued. Typical was the experience of Harold Kohr, whose office was on the first floor of the DPC building, across the street from the Ad building. Somehow, to his own amazement, Kohr found himself on the outside of the building, having escaped through a narrow 18-inch window without a scratch or a tear in his clothing. In Administration and Engineering buildings, window glass popped everywhere.

Harold Mansfield's secretary had recently suffered a broken leg in a skiing accident. While the whole Administration Building started to shake, she, being a sensible girl and versed in earthquake technique, made a dive under her desk. When Mansfield dashed from his office to check the welfare of his secretary, all he could see was a leg encased in plaster, sticking out from under the desk. It was rather significant that all executives' first thought seemed to be of their secretaries. But then, real good secretaries are hard to come by.

On the third floor, Dora Hunter's boss, Wellwood Beall, happened to be out of town. When the quake hit, Dora dashed into Beall's office.

"Then I remembered that one was supposed to stand in a doorway," Dora recalls. "I ran back and stood in the hall doorway. Just then Lysle Wood came by, hurrying to get upstairs in the Engineering Building, to check on his secretary. I grabbed him and wouldn't let him go. As soon as the earthquake subsided, he continued on to his office. Later in the afternoon the phone rang and it was Mr. Wood. He said, 'That was so much fun I'd like to make a date with you for the next earthquake.'"

My office was on the first floor of the Ad building. Its windows were shaded by canvas awnings. Glass from the floor above fell outward and down, shredding the awnings. The glass from my windows came inward, covering my desk and conference table.

The office of Bill Allen, Boeing president, was on the third floor. Not a window in his office was so much as cracked. "They wouldn't dare" was the general consensus.

When the after-shocks ceased and excitement subsided, the cafeteria was a glorious mess. No one could remember where he had been seated. A crew was brought in to clear the tray-and-dish-covered tables. Most workers forgot about lunch and returned to work to compare experiences with fellow workers.

Just as some people in Seattle date major events from the great fire of '89 or the snow of '16, others now date from the quake of '49.

2

The Press

Reporters run the gamut—excellent to pains in the derriere

No Baby— Dealing with the press is an interesting and perhaps the most challenging aspect of public relations. Reporters of every conceivable type were to be found among the media with whom we dealt. There were completely ignorant reporters who hardly knew the empennage of an airplane from the under-carriage. Then there were the astute reporters such as Dick Witkin of the *New York Times*, Marvin Miles of the *Los Angeles Times*, Al Hughes of the *Christian Science Monitor*, Wayne Thomis of the *Chicago Tribune*, Lev Richards of the Portland *Oregonian*, and Bob Twiss of the *Seattle Times*.

There were reporters who came up with long lists of studied, provocative questions that took real research to answer. Then there were the headaches, the real pains in the derriere, fortunately only a few, who came with preconceived ideas and wanted their premises proved.

One such was a girl reporter from the old *Life* magazine. She came from New York with all the studied assurance of a New Yorker, backed by a photographer, to do a story on women workers in the war effort. We cooperated to the extent permitted by war-time security. Then she came up with what was to be the pièce-de-résistance of her story.

"Now I want to get a picture of a father going to work on the night shift while his wife is coming off the day shift. I want to show him handing over their baby to the wife. He goes to work, she goes home to take care of the baby after doing her bit. Great story!"

"I've never seen nor heard of such an occurrence," I told her. "But I'll check with the guards and ask if any of them ever saw a baby exchanged at shift change."

"I just know that with all these people there must be some couples exchanging babies," she argued. "I'm going to watch for myself!" She spent two days standing around at shift changes. No luck.

I was afraid she might try to stage the picture by inducing some couple to cooperate in a phony setup. Fortunately our people were too smart to fall for such a proposal.

✈ ✈ ✈ ✈ ✈

P.R. Crap—Rollout of Boeing's first jumbo jet 747 was a major event in company and aviation history. To mark it, a special program had been arranged. Guests included executives from major airlines around the world. And, of course, the press was included. Major newspapers and other media, both domestic and foreign, assigned their top writers for the event.

Among the well-known writers was Bob Considine, covering for I.N.S. (International News Service). Bob informed us he was on a tight schedule. He was booked for a talk at a Tacoma breakfast meeting. The 747 rollout was set for 11 a.m.

I arranged for my brother Al, an experienced pilot, to pick up Bob in Tacoma, hop over to Boeing Field, pick me up and then fly on to Everett and the rollout.

On the way north I briefed Considine on salient facts of the Everett plant and the 747. Largest plant in the world by volume; 47 acres under one roof; the three doors spanning production bays were each as long as a football field; the 747 could carry up to 450 passengers, etc.

"Pure P.R. crap, my friend," Bob observed indifferently. We landed, rushed to the rollout. Everything went as scheduled.

The next morning I scanned the *Post-Intelligencer*, Considine's outlet in Seattle. There, almost word for word in his story was my "P.R. crap."

In public relations we don't care what you call it, just so you quote us correctly.

✈ ✈ ✈ ✈ ✈

P.R. Headache—Taxi testing is an integral part of the overall testing of any new plane developed at Boeing. Thus final check of brakes, controls, acceleration and ground handling was being conducted on the first production Flying Fortress, the YB-17. John

Corkvielle and Stanley Ulmstead, Air Corps pilots, were at the controls this spring day in the late '30s.

The B-17 was a three-point tail-dragger with a tail wheel instead of the nose wheel common to today's aircraft. In a test of quick stopping from high speed taxi, the YB-17's brakes froze and locked. Although almost stopped, the plane rotated on its landing gear, tail high in the air, nose ignobly on the ground. An ungainly and unsightly position for Boeing's latest pride.

Quickly sensing the potential for adverse publicity, Harold Mansfield, company public relations manager, rushed over to Fred Laudan, factory manager. "Fred, you've got to get that tail pulled down and the plane righted in 15 minutes or there will be pictures in every major newspaper in the country," Mansfield warned.

Laudan explained very carefully that this was the first production model; that you just didn't yank the tail of the plane back to the ground. He wasn't going to take any chance of damaging the aircraft beyond the slight damage to the nose.

Somehow, as it always does, word got out, and within Mansfield's 15 minutes local newspaper photographers arrived. Their pictures, as predicted, appeared nationally.

You will find very few public relations men, even youthful ones, without a few gray hairs.

✈ ✈ ✈ ✈ ✈

No News—Robert L. (Bob) Twiss of the *Seattle Times* was generally regarded as one of the most astute aviation editors in the U.S. He had personal friends among practically all the airline presidents of the world and was on a first-name basis with many of them.

One of Boeing's early sales of the 707 was to Aer Lingus, the Irish airline. As customary, Boeing left announcement of the sale to its customer. Meantime, super secrecy in regard to the transaction was the order of the day.

Jim Boynton, then of the news bureau at headquarters, received a phone call from Twiss.

"How's everything, Jim? Any developments I might be interested in down there at the plant?"

"No, not a thing I can think of, Bob," Jim replied, crossing his fingers to atone for the little white lie.

"No recent sales, no announcements coming up shortly?"

"No, nothing in the works, Bob," Jim lied again, torn between being truthful and the admonition for secrecy on the Irish deal.

"Okay, Jim, Erin go braugh," Bob replied with a slyness which could be sensed over the telephone.

✈ ✈ ✈ ✈ ✈

First 737 Sale—When Boeing announced its commitment to the two-engine 737 program, the key question was which airline would make the first purchase. A group of Boeing salesmen was in Cologne, Germany, conferring with Gerhard Hoeltje, president of Lufthansa Airline.

As indicated earlier, Bob Twiss was on a first name basis with a number of airline presidents, including Herr Hoeltje. Sensing the possibility of an announcement, Twiss phoned Hoeltje and said, "Gerhard, is it correct that you will start off the 737 program by announcing purchase of 20 or 21 planes?"

Hoeltje told Twiss to wait, that he would have to

go into another office. There, while the Boeing salesmen waited outside, Hoeltje confirmed that the purchase would be made.

Twiss ran the story; "It was learned today that Lufthansa, the German airline, will kick off the Boeing 737 program by announcing purchase of 20 or 21 planes." The article went on to detail the plane and its potential. Bill Schultze, aviation reporter on the rival Seattle *Post-Intelligencer*, on reading the *Times* story, immediately phoned the local Lufthansa representative who said he knew nothing about the purchase. The *P-I* ran a story denying the *Times* story. It made a correction the next day when official announcement came from Germany.

✈ ✈ ✈ ✈ ✈

Headache—This rivalry between the two newspapers was a headache to the public relations department and officials at Boeing. Company policy was to treat all media as equally as possible. The wide contacts Twiss had with the military and airlines, plus the time advantage enjoyed by an afternoon newspaper on the West Coast, gave the *Times* a decided break on most stories. Contributing to the situation was Boeing's policy of leaving it to the customers to announce all purchases.

Charley Lindeman, then publisher of the *P-I*, complained to Bill Allen one day, "What do we have to do to get a break on some of these stories?" Allen replied, "Hire Twiss."

✈ ✈ ✈ ✈ ✈

Korean Xmas—It was during the Korean war. The *Chicago Tribune* initiated a fund-raising program to buy Christmas gifts for Illinois residents serving in the Far-East conflict. My friend, Wayne Thomis, aviation editor of the *Tribune*, was given the task of making the Christmas purchases.

Arriving in Seattle, Wayne asked me to join him on some of his buying forays. His purchase objectives were warm clothing—mittens, gloves, sweaters, caps, etc., and special treats for the Christmas holidays.

At the candy counter of the Frederick and Nelson department store, Wayne said: "I would like to sample some of your chocolates." After biting into several, he continued, "I'd like a ton of this one, a ton of that, two tons of the brittle." The gape-mouthed clerk needed real persuasion that it was not a joke. At the bakery— four tons of fruitcake.

Finally, in time to catch the last boat that would reach Korea before Christmas, all of Wayne's purchases were completed, packaged, and placed aboard. We held a sort of victory dinner—objective achieved.

The next morning I got another call from Wayne. "The office just wired another $50,000 in last minute contributions. I've got to spend it." More of the "I'll take a ton of that" routine, trucks were hired to rush the final purchases to Vancouver where they caught the last-chance boat for Korea.

I'm sure there were a lot of warm and sweet-sated far-from-home Illinois soldiers that Christmas.

✈ ✈ ✈ ✈ ✈

Foreign Press Visits—To keep the world press familiar with Boeing and its products, it has long been the practice to bring representatives of foreign media on visits to Boeing operations in the Seattle and Wichita areas. Since most of the visitors had layovers in New York on their way to Seattle, it was one of Mark Nevils' duties to meet and guide the visitors during their one- or two-day stops in the East.

One such visiting media group was from South Africa. Four represented the Afrikaans press, the other four, English papers and radio. The party was led by a stern Afrikaanser. He indicated to Nevils that they would like to visit the *New York Times Magazine*. They were very critical of some of the articles published in the *Magazine*.

Mark called Lester Markel, the *Magazine* editor, and arranged an appointment. A lively debate ensued. The South Africans accused the *Times* authors of being biased, second rate, inexperienced journalists. Markel stoutly defended the integrity of his authors. Nevils doubted that minds were changed on either side, but the South Africans enjoyed the interview and declared it a feature of their New York visit.

The group came on to Seattle, arriving on July 3. What to do to entertain them on the Fourth of July? Elmer Vogel, head of the public relations news bureau, and I took the group in two company station wagons. We drove first to Grand Coulee dam, which suitably impressed the visitors. We then went on to Nespelem on the Colville Indian Reservation where the Indians were holding their annual 10-day celebration. The South Africans were particularly interested in the Indians and amazed that they were not required to have identification cards and could come and go as they pleased. On to Chesaw (the only town in the U.S. named for a Chinese) where a community rodeo was being held. Then down to Oroville where State Senator Hallauer, a friend of Vogel's, had arranged a barbecue supper. As we left for an overnight stay in Penticton, British Columbia, one of the Oroville ladies who had assisted at the barbecue, impulsively threw her arms around the stern leader and gave him a resounding kiss. The other members of the party declared their certainty that it was the first time he had been kissed by a woman in at least 30 years.

✈ ✈ ✈ ✈ ✈

The King's English—A common, universal language? Not necessarily so. Americans have learned not to use the word "bum" in England nor to ask for a cookie in South Africa.

In Sydney, Australia, a Boeing official entered a taxi at his hotel in the King's Cross area and asked to be driven to the "A and P" building, as many Americans referred to the Australian and Pacific building.

"Never heard of it," the taxi driver said.

"It's one of your main buildings. How long have you been driving taxi?"

"Ten years."

"Well, go ahead downtown and I'll show you where it is." Just off King's Way the Boeing man said, "That's it, right there around the corner."

"Aye, mite," the driver exclaimed, "you had me there. You meant the aye and pie building."

The Boeing man not only learned the Australian pronunciation of "A" and "P", he also learned that the part of a plane at the rear is the "tile."

✈ ✈ ✈ ✈ ✈

Scotch Shoes—Among countries from which newsmen came to visit Boeing were Israel, Australia, England, France, Germany, Ireland, Pakistan, India and South Africa. The visit of the group from South Africa has already been recounted.

In a *mea culpa* confession we will have to admit to certain gaffes in accommodating these various groups.

On a Friday we made the error of arranging a roast beef dinner for the Irish press visitors. Fortunately, fish was available on the menu. One of the Irishmen was already in a dour mood. The evening before, following European custom, he had placed his shoes outside the door of his room so they could be polished. Some playful American, no doubt a bit tiddly, had poured whiskey into them. Unfortunately, it was the only pair of shoes the visitor had brought with him. It was three reeking hours after breakfast before the stores opened and we could get him a new pair.

✈ ✈ ✈ ✈ ✈

Unhappy Visitor—Usually the visitors returned home on the flight of a plane being delivered to their national airline. Sometimes delays occurred and public relations was hard put to fill in the unexpected hours or days.

Faced with such a situation, Elmer Vogel, News Bureau Chief, had a solution. Before joining Boeing, he had been head of the Associated Press office in Olympia, the state capital. He made arrangements for the delayed visiting group (their nation shall not be identified) to observe the legislature in session and then to visit the governor. One of the newsmen had displayed an unhappy mien from the beginning. He didn't like his companions, the station wagon transporting them to Olympia was not posh enough, and he didn't like the food. Shortly after 2 o'clock he announced that he had to be back in Seattle for an appointment at 5 p.m. The date with the governor, including refreshments, was set for 4 p.m., and all other newsmen of the party had indicated real pleasure with the proposed program.

"Our friend insisted, however, that I take him back to Seattle (60 miles from Olympia) and to hell with our previous plans," Vogel relates. "Instead, I took him to the Greyhound bus station, bought him a ticket and arranged with the driver to drop him off at Boeing headquarters. Our guest was furious and still objecting angrily when I 'helped' him board the bus.

"When I rejoined the group, I was greeted with cheers and hand clapping. I heard no more of the problem's solution until some time later I received a letter from the man who had been so upset. It contained a profuse apology and a rare one-pound note of his country. He said he had noted that I was a collector and hoped the note would help atone for his actions."

✦ ✦ ✦ ✦ ✦

Again Vogel was in charge of a visiting press group, this time from Australia. The 12 jolly Aussies were to return home on a Qantas delivery flight. Over a hot weekend Vogel arranged a trip to Mt. Rainier. Aware of the Australian propensity for keeping the whistle wet, Vogel had stocked the two station wagons with a generous supply of beer, kept cool with a substantial supply of ice.

"We weren't more than 10 miles south of Renton on the Maple Valley road to Enumclaw when our guests noted the beer and a concurrent thirstiness," Vogel relates. "We pulled over to the side of the road and started handling out the stubbies. The first Aussie to taste his beer sputtered and exclaimed in disgust, "This stuff is cold!" The others joined in voicing a decided objection to American cold beer.

"They solved the problem by lining up the bottles on the hoods of the station wagons in the sun and waited for a proper 'warming.' Many goggle-eyed passing motorists slowed to get another look at the 'Boeing Brewery' at roadside, until the Aussies decided the beer was at a drinkable temperature."

✈ ✈ ✈ ✈ ✈

I experienced the other side of the coin in Sydney, Australia. It was two days before Christmas and the peak of the summer below the Equator. The temperature was near 100 degrees, so at lunch I asked the waitress for iced coffee.

"I don't know if there is any cooled coffee in the kitchen," she said. I instructed her "Just bring me a bowl of ice, a glass with a spoon in it, and a pot of hot coffee."

She did as asked and was about to pour the coffee into the bowl of ice when I stopped her. I then filled the glass with ice, put the spoon in, and topped the glass with coffee. All over the dining room heads were turned, and it was obvious they were saying, "Look what that crazy Yank is doing!"

Okay, my good Australian friends, you can have your coffee hot and your beer warm. In warm weather we will take them both cold.

3

Manion

The unique, uninhibited, ever-smiling Vern,
only one of his kind

He Shot Queens—Vern Manion, photographer, shot queens and peasants, Arabian sheiks, presidents, airline officials and pilots until his retirement in 1983. He spent more than 5,000 hours in the air on aerial photography missions.

Stocky, gregarious, ever-smiling, Vern undoubtedly knew, and was known by, more Boeing employees than any other person in the company. He could charm the most sour puss into a photogenic smile, induce pilots to give him "just five minutes more" during photo flights, order Bill Allen, Boeing president, to take various poses and in general established himself as a Boeing legend. He flew all over the world accompanying demonstration flights of various Boeing aircraft. He declared that Russia and China were the only two countries in the world over which he hadn't flown.

A book could hardly encompass all the stories told about Manion and the stories he, himself, tells. Justice will hardly be done him in this single chapter.

✈ ✈ ✈ ✈ ✈

Shortly after the outbreak of World War II Vern left his job at Boeing and enlisted in the U.S. Navy as a Photographer Mate. His first assignment, after boot camp, was to the naval base at San Diego.

Soon after his arrival there a meeting of Pacific area top brass was convened at the base. A group picture of the various admirals—full, vice and rear— captains and commodores was ordered. Manion drew the assignment to make the shot.

The group assembled on the steps of one of the administration buildings. At one end of the first row was a full admiral, gold sleeve-stripes gleaming. Sighting through his camera, Manion decided that the group was too spread out.

"Hey, sailor, you on the end," he called to the admiral. "Step in a bit closer."

The group stiffened to rigid attention, expecting a reprimand for the brash young photographer, then relaxed as the admiral laughed and moved as directed.

✈ ✈ ✈ ✈ ✈

Manion Meets Sheiks—After his military service Manion returned to Boeing and his old job. One of his assignments was to accompany the 727 on a demonstration flight to Jedda, Saudi Arabia. Before the plane landed, Manion was warned that the sheiks did not like to be photographed; in fact, cameras were not permitted.

Disconsolate, Vern stood in the plane's shade, viewing the colorful assemblage of white-robed sheiks and mentally planning the shots he would like to make. As he stood, disappointed, hands in pockets, one of the sheiks came up to him. "You look very unhappy," the sheik said. "Is something wrong?"

"I'm the Boeing photographer, and they tell me I can't take any pictures," Manion replied, plainly expressing his frustration. "Wait here," the sheik directed.

He soon returned. "Get your camera," he said. "All right to take pictures. I will escort you." And one of old Ibn Saud's numerous sons took Manion in tow.

Enlargements of many of the shots Manion made, in full color, grace numerous offices of the oil-rich country, which is one of Boeing's best airplane customers.

✈ ✈ ✈ ✈ ✈

Wolfe's Longjohns—Never miss the chance for a shot was Manion's motto. Air Force General Wolfe had been in Alaska on a winter inspection trip. In respect of the weather he had accoutered himself with red longjohn underwear, heavy parka and similar gear. On return to the lower states the general, still wearing his winter gear, landed at Boeing Field and came to the Boeing Administration Building lobby to await transportation. He sat on a leather lounge, a generous expanse of red showing between trouser cuffs and shoe tops.

Manion, camera in hand, happened to walk through the lobby. Spying the general, whom he knew from previous visits, he decided it was an opportunity for a picture. He peered through his view-finder, did a bit of lens adjustment, noted the exposed red underwear, and paused.

"Say, General, would you mind standing up and pulling down your pants?" When the receptionist broke up, the general joined in the laughter. No one ever took umbrage with Manion.

✈   ✈   ✈   ✈   ✈

Control Problem—To get a head-on shot of the six-engine B-47 bomber in flight required considerable ingenuity. A B-25 was selected as photo plane, as it was one of the few planes that could keep ahead of the B-47. Removal of the B-25 tail cone left a large opening from which to make the head-on shots.

On the day of the flight Manion and his camera, and a motion picture crew with its equipment, put their gear at the rear of the plane and took improvised seats. As the plane accelerated for take-off, the cameras started to slide toward the gaping hole in the tail. Manion jumped to the rear, grabbed the cameras and pulled them back. At that moment the plane rotated for take-off and Manion found himself sliding toward that yawning opening. He grabbed out instinctively with both hands.

The plane continued to climb, even more steeply. "I've got a control problem here," the pilot radioed to the Boeing control tower. "I'm coming around to land." On the ground the pilot explained, "I couldn't get the nose down. I cranked in full deflection and had to get the co-pilot on the yoke with me."

Manion bravely confessed that his considerable bulk had been at the extreme rear of the plane. Further that he had a very firm grip, in fact, a lock on the elevator control cables which he had grabbed as he slid toward the opening. Being Manion, he was forgiven. With cameras properly stowed and photographer weight distributed, the spectacular shot was made without further incident.

✈ ✈ ✈ ✈ ✈

LeMay's Cigar—Aerial refueling of fighter and bomber aircraft came into use shortly after World War II as a means of extending the range of both types. One system, "hose and drogue," employed a flexible hose from the tanker plane with which the refueling plane made connection. The Boeing system was based on a "flying boom," a telescoping series of pipes which literally were "flown" from the tanker to a connection with the thirsty plane below.

In the early stages of perfecting the system, a platform was erected at the north end of Boeing Field and one of the "flying booms" installed there for tests of fuel flow, maneuverability, etc., and for use in training the in-flight operators.The gasoline supply on the platform would be forced through the boom and into a receptacle below as the boom was "flown" in various tests. Considerable spillage of fuel was experienced as the tests went on.

General Curtis LeMay, the cigar-chomping curmudgeon general, known as one of the toughest (and most able) in the Air Force, came to Seattle one day to witness tests of the new refueling method, as it was of vital importance to him and the Strategic Air Command.

With an entourage of company and Air Force officials, LeMay was at the test stand. Manion, the versatile photographer, was present to record the general's visit. Sighting through his camera, Manion, aware of the liberal amount of spilled gasoline on the ground, noticed with consternation the general's lit cigar. Lowering his camera, he shouted, "Hey, General, put out that goddamn cigar." Possibly LeMay had never been so addressed before. Startled, he took the cigar from his mouth, looked around until he found a dry spot which the gasoline had not reached and stomped out his cigar without comment.

✈ ✈ ✈ ✈ ✈

Pantsed—Tex, famed Boeing test pilot, and Colonel Guy Townsend, Air Force representative, flew hundreds of hours with Manion as a passenger or directing their maneuvers from a photography plane.

"All right, Tex, move in a little closer," Manion would direct over the command radio. "Now how about you guys peeling off sharply so I can get an under shot?"

"We're going to get you some day, Manion," the two pilots bantered with their favorite photographer.

That day arrived after a long photo session in the air and follow-up on the ground, when Manion had the two in and out of their high-altitude pressure equipment. Looking at Tex, with a nod at Manion, Townsend said, "Tex, let's pants him!"

The two grabbed Manion and a wild struggle ensued. Manion fighting for his honor put up a real battle. "We got his pants down over his knees, but he finally got away from us," Tex Johnston reports. "We'll get you another time," Townsend vowed.

Being pantsed was a manifestation of the affection in which Manion was held. It was really a bit of an honor.

✈ ✈ ✈ ✈ ✈

No Linguist—Despite roaming the world on assignments, foreign ways and languages were a source of bewilderment to Manion. On duty with a group of Boeing representatives at the Paris Air Show, Manion was having petit déjeuner (he insisted it was breakfast) in his room. Wanting more butter, he decided to try his limited French. He rang room service and asked for "deux buerre." A moment later a waiter arrived with two bottles of beer. Beurre-bierre. Manion never did master French pronunciation.

✈ ✈ ✈

Germany provided equal bewilderment for Boeing's popular photographer. Coming from a hot day at the airport, Manion jumped into the tub for a refreshing, relaxing bath. As he half reclined in the soothing water, he noticed a tasseled cord hanging beside the tub. He gave it a tentative inquisitorial pull.

Shortly the door opened and in walked the maid. While Manion shrieked "Nien, nien!" she calmly prepared to wash his back, since she had been summoned by the cord to do just that. All in the day's work for her. Manion learned not to pull cords unless you knew what they were for.

✈ ✈ ✈

Ham and . . . Foreign practices and language continued to plague Manion. Again in Paris he ordered ham and eggs for breakfast, (no more of this petit déjeuner business). He pronounced the words distinctly and shaped his fingers into an oval to indicate an egg. The waiter brought him corn flakes. "Not corn flakes," Manion protested, "ham and eggs!" Pointing firmly at the corn flakes, the waiter declared "Ham and eggs!"

✈ ✈ ✈ ✈ ✈

Only Noodles—On one of his assigned forays overseas, Manion was in Rome with a Boeing military test crew. General Arnold Luehman, bon vivant, happened to encounter the Boeing group and extolled to them the reputation of the fettucini featured in a certain restaurant in the old part of Rome.

"Best in Rome, which means the best in Italy, which means the best in the world," Luehman declared. Proudly he guided several of the Boeing party—Manion included—to the praised restaurant. When the pièce-de-résistance arrived, Luehman awaited the anticipated praise.

Manion forked a bit of the pasta. "Hey, this ain't nothing but noodles!" he declared.

✈ ✈ ✈ ✈ ✈

Dull Day—A neighbor, who lived a few houses away, rode with Manion most mornings as far as Plant Two. There he took the bus to his prosaic and tedious repetitious tasks at a desk, while Manion went on to the day's challenges.

One morning on leaving the car, he asked, "What are you going to do today, Vern?"

"Gee, I don't know. I'll go in and look at the hook and see what's up."

The next morning the neighbor asked, "Well,

what did you do yesterday?"

"Oh, I made a few prints, then I flew up to Greenland and back."

"And all I did was sit at that desk and concentrate on a little space in front of me. I'm going to quit!" Manion's friend declared.

The man carried out the threat. Invested in a small apartment house, then parlayed that into substantial real estate holdings in downtown Seattle.

Apparently Manion's casual report of a flight to Greenland set his neighbor on a new track in life.

✈ ✈ ✈ ✈ ✈

Momentous!—First flight of the prototype for America's first jet passenger transport—Boeing's Dash-80 which became the 707.

Manion was to supervise the in-flight photography. The photographers from the wire services, national magazines and local papers were put aboard a Boeing Stratotanker. Manion took his place at the refueling-boom operator's window at the rear.

After his preliminary testing, Tex Johnston, the test pilot, brought the Dash-80 up toward the Stratotanker and reported via the command radio, "Manion, no pictures, I have lost hydraulic power and can't get the gear or flaps up."

"Tex, we got to get pictures. We have all these press people aboard, we can't tell 'em no pics."

"Manion, you can't show the plane with all the gear and the flaps down."

"All right, Tex, tell you what you do. You come up behind and under me, and I'll shoot down on you—the gear won't show."

"What about the flaps?"

"To hell with the flaps."

Tex moved in behind and below the tanker, Manion talking to him. "All right, up just a bit. Now come ahead a few feet. I can still see the nose gear. Good."

"Just one shot, Manion. I don't want to hold this."

"Two shots! One color, one black and white. I've got them."

"As soon as we got on the ground, I rushed to the lab and developed the color shot," Manion says. "I gave the wet negative to the *Life* photographer, who took off for the airport. *Life* had arranged to have a plane held for 15 minutes. The *Life* man held that negative out the window of the car to dry, as he sped down the highway. Rushed to New York, Manion's shot resulted in a full color, double-page, center-spread in *Life* just three days later.

When copies of *Life* were received, Allen called Manion to his office. "Vern, I was listening to the conversation between you and Tex. You persuaded him to make that shot. Then I heard you telling him up or down, ahead and back. I should have fired you and would have if you hadn't come up with a terrific publicity shot for the company."

Since a bleed, full color, double-spread, center-page page in *Life* cost well over $150,000, one had to admit that Manion did a fair day's work.

✈ ✈ ✈ ✈ ✈

First Delivery—Some airline customers, particularly those from foreign countries, made considerable ceremony of taking delivery of their first aircraft. Formal, and in some cases, religious ceremonies marked the occasion.

The supervisor in charge of the flight line on such

occasions was a chap by the name of Ed Cohen. When Aer Lingus, Irish airline dignitaries, arrived at the delivery site, they were accompanied by the local Catholic bishop.

"It ain't going to do you fellows any good, I've already blessed it," Cohen declared.

Manion was on hand to record the ceremony when El Al, official Israelian airline, received its first aircraft. In this case, a rabbi was to perform the ceremonies. Cohen was most cooperative.

"Hey, Rabbi," Manion asked, "who's going to cut the ribbon?"

The rabbi broke into laughter.

✈ ✈ ✈ ✈ ✈

Chased by a B-52—A unique cross-wind landing gear was one of the many "first-time" features of the B-52 eight-jet bomber. In cross-wind landings the body of the airplane could be pointed directly into the wind at an angle to the runway. The landing gear, however, could be rotated, so that it would point straight down the center of the runway.

Manion drew the assignment to make a picture of the B-52 in its "crabbed," cross-wind position. The plan was for Tex Johnston to taxi the 52 slowly while Manion, sitting on the tailgate of a station wagon driven just ahead, would make his shots.

"The driver of the station wagon was too far ahead of the 52," Manion relates. "I kept yelling at him to slow down, but he saw all that airplane on his tail and sped up instead. I jumped off and stood in the middle of the runway shooting. I looked up and that plane was getting awfully close. I couldn't run to either side because of the huge wing span of a B-52. So

I start to run down the runway. Behind me I heard the engines being revved up and down. That damn Tex Johnston was chasing me with a B-52! Out of breath, I managed to catch up with the station wagon and climb aboard. I think Tex was still laughing in the cockpit."

✈ ✈ ✈ ✈ ✈

Money-Making Deal—Eddie Rickenbacher, famed auto racer, World War I ace, and president of Eastern Air Lines was a passenger on the Dash-80 on a flight from Seattle to Baltimore.

"I was kept busy shooting people who wanted their picture taken with Rickenbacher," Manion says in recalling another of his experiences. "Finally Rickenbacher said, 'No more pictures. Anyone that wants a picture has got to pay me a dollar.' And he collected a half dozen or more. Didn't offer to split with me.

"On a 747 flight from Singapore to Taiwan, we had Madam Chennault, wife of General Chennault of Flying Tigers fame, aboard. People wanted their picture taken with her. So I told her how Rickenbacher had charged a dollar for each picture.

"'Good,' she said. 'We will charge $2. One for me and one for you.' Made several dollars with my partner."

✈ ✈ ✈ ✈ ✈

Dash-80 Retired—After several hundred hours of test and demonstration flying, the Dash-80 was flown east and presented to the Smithsonian Institution for its aviation collection.

Following the formal presentation, the Boeing representatives continued on to New York, where a party, commemorating the occasion, was held at the 21 Club. Manion, of course, was along to record all the proceedings.

"I wanted to get an overall shot of the large group as they sat around tables in 21. To do so, I climbed up and stood on the bar for the best angle" (Manion would do that.) "There wasn't too much light, so I warned everyone not to move while I took a timed shot. Just when I opened the lens, my foot slipped into a sink full of chipped ice. I didn't dare move, so I stood there with one foot nearly frozen."

He got the shot.

Unfortunately, the Smithsonian's planned great aviation hall has not been built. As a result the Dash-80, together with a number of other historic aircraft, sits on the open desert at an air base just outside Tucson, Arizona.

It would be great if the Dash-80, like the 100 could come home to Seattle and take an honored place in the Museum of Flight.

✈ ✈ ✈ ✈ ✈

By Just Gets By—By Wingett was the second of Boeing's trio of public relations photographers. His most harrowing experience occurred at the 13,500-foot altitude airport at LaPaz, Bolivia, the highest commercial airport in the world. The 727 was there to demonstrate its high altitude performance capabilities.

Wingett rounded up an ancient truck, several Indian girls in their derby hats and a couple of llamas to lend color to his shots.

"I was at the end of the runway shooting landings

and take-offs," Wingett tells of his experience. "Jack Waddell, the pilot, turned on the landing lights to indicate the last landing and for me to come back to the plane. The truck sputtered along at 10 miles an hour.

"When I got to the vicinity of the 727, it was surrounded by a mob of Bolivians and Indians. I was trying to fight my way through the throng with my heavy equipment. Suddenly I saw the plane start to taxi slowly away and the landing stairs, at the rear, began to retract.

"Without any money or extra clothing and not speaking the language, I wasn't about to be left there. I finally fought through the crowd and ran after the plane. I managed to grasp the edge of the landing stairs as it was about halfway up. Someone pulled me into the plane."

Wingett collapsed to the floor after the exertion at the extreme high altitude. He was put on pure oxygen and recovered after a short time.

He later learned that Waddell had to start the plane taxiing as the brakes were not cooling properly in the high altitude, and he was afraid that they might "freeze."

✈ ✈ ✈ ✈ ✈

Not Protocol—Vern Rutledge, who with By Wingett, completed the photographer troika, learned a lesson in caution during a demonstration tour of the 707 to Paraguay, South America. Ever alert for the best shot, he innocently stepped between the head of state and his bodyguards. Vern suddenly found himself lifted off his feet and unceremoniously set to one side.

On the same tour it took the intercession of the

flight crew to get Rutledge back on the airplane. Overzealous local gendarmes in Buenos Aires, Argentina, thought he was just another photographer trying to slip aboard the aircraft. Fortunately, two of the crew saw his plight and went to his rescue.

✈ ✈ ✈ ✈ ✈

40 Below Shots—Before the advent of pressurized aircraft, Boeing photographers wore heavy flight suits and shot from open doorways and hatches. Temperatures as low as 40 below might be experienced in the aircraft at altitude. When it was learned that they were working from open doorways without safety belts, an order was issued, "Safety belts must be worn at all times when camera plane doors and hatches are removed for shooting."

On all photo flights radio communication established cooperation between the photographers and the aircraft they were shooting. One Air Force pilot, Colonel Harold Hansen, now a Seattle businessman, even assisted the photographers. "Okay, Manion, I think you should shoot this at f.18 at 500. Shutter cocked? Here I come. Hit it."

✈ ✈ ✈ ✈ ✈

F.D.R. Drops In—Dewey Dewees, account executive on the Boeing advertising account with N.W. Ayer and Son, agency, was conversing one day in the Administration lobby with Dorothy Kuljis, receptionist. There seemed to be considerable bustle and rushing about. As it increased, Dewey casually remarked, "What's all the excitement? You would think it was the President." Glancing out the door, he exclaimed, "My god, it is the President!"

F.D.R. had flown in to Seattle unannounced and was on an unheralded visit to the Boeing plant which was turning out B-17s at an unprecedented rate.

Word of the President's visit spread rapidly, and Vern Manion, ever alert, was one of the first to respond. Grabbing his camera, he rushed through the lobby to the building steps below which F.D.R. sat in an open car.

Raising his camera, Manion was about to shoot a picture when a burly Secret Service man grabbed his arm, twisted it behind his back and commanded, "Drop the camera!" "The heck I will," Manion replied indignantly. "If I drop it, I'll break it and Old Scrooge won't buy another." It was one of the few times that Manion didn't get his shot.

I didn't mind his calling me "Scrooge," but I did object to the "old."

✈   ✈   ✈   ✈   ✈

Boeing photographers agree their most difficult photo assignment was shooting a mixed formation of airplanes—a B-17, B-29, B-47 and a B-52. The four, together with the KC-97 photo plane rendezvoused over Seattle.

The B-17 had to fly at full throttle, while the B-52 lumbered along at near stalling speed in order to keep any kind of formation. Finally, proper formation was briefly achieved over northern California, some 600 miles to the south of Seattle.

The shot was spectacular and attained wide usage.

✈   ✈   ✈   ✈   ✈

Old Is Best—Speed Graphics, Mamiyas, Nikon, Pentaxes were among cameras used by Boeing photographers. A favorite was a 30-year-old 4 by 5 Graflex which "turned out as good results as any," according to Manion. "Besides, it was handy to sit on," he added.

4

Front Desk— Receptionists

Those "See All, Hear All, Say Nothing"
Receptionists

Guardians of the Portals—The receptionists at the Boeing headquarters building on Seattle's East Marginal Way were, and are, key contributors in the company's operations.

It is their duty to welcome and smooth the way for important visitors or those who have legitimate business with the company. At the same time, using tact and inherent intuition, they have to turn aside those who have no appointments. On occasion, with little white lies, they protect executives from intrusions.

Three who served in this key spot at headquarters during my time with the company were Alice Mustoe, Dorothy Kuljis and Barbara Loar. Barbara is typical of those who, like St. Peter and with almost as much authority, stood guard at the gate. With keen wit and sharp memory she has passed along some of her experiences.

Very seldom did the receptionists have to call on guards for assistance in handling obstreperous individuals who asserted they were going to gain entrance to some particular office come hell or high water. Because of their working relationship, the guards took delight in playing jokes on whatever receptionist presided in the Administration Building.

One day a man stumbled his way to the guard at Gate 18 and asked to be directed to the employment office. He reeked of garlic which permeated even the open air surrounding the guard gate. Holtby, the guard, could see that the man was no candidate for employment. Then, with inner glee, he directed the man: "Go to the main headquarters building, back toward town. The building with a curved driveway in front. You go in there, up close to the desk and ask the young lady there. She can direct you to the employment office."

"He nearly bowled me over when he came through the door in a haze of garlic," Barbara says. "I got rid of him as quickly as possible, and even opening the outside doors and a generous application of room freshener didn't air out the lobby for some time."

✦ ✦ ✦

On one occasion Barbara had a parcel of visitor badges to take to the reception desk in the 201 building, across 16th Avenue South from main Plant Two. She jumped into her car, and knowing Omsby, the guard at the gate to the 201 building, she drove through without stopping. Omsby jumped into his car, touched the siren, and with blue lights flashing, stopped Barbara.

"Out of the car. Hands on hood," he ordered. Then he pat-searched the fuming young lady. "Now open the trunk of your car."

"Omsby, I'm going to kill you for this," Barbara averred.

"Okay. But think how much fun the people watching this are having," Omsby replied, releasing his "prisoner."

✈ ✈ ✈

Earlier when working in the communication center, Barbara had, on occasion, to pick up material at the print shop in one of the annex buildings south of the main plant. On the way she usually took a shortcut through the jig erection shop. (For those not familiar with manufacturing processes, a jig is a tool, a form, in which parts are assembled. Some are small, others are substantial steel structures, erecting of which requires a large construction area.)

As Barbara was on a pick-up errand one day, a worker noted her taking her usual shortcut and asked her where she was going.

"After a layout," she replied.

When she returned, the same man said, with a bit of a leer,"Well, did you get your layout when you took the shortcut?"

"Yes, and I didn't even muss my hair," Barbara replied coolly.

✈ ✈ ✈

It was, as they say in fiction, a dark and rainy day. In front of the Administration Building a county engineering crew was working on a problem connected with the storm. One of the crew, a young lady, was working down in a manhole.

She emerged rather hastily and made her way to the building entrance. Like the men of the crew she wore heavy rubber boots, "tin pants" held up by heavy suspenders, knee-length waterproof coat and a tin helmet.

Entering the Ad building lobby, she hurriedly asked Barbara, who presided at the reception desk, "Could I please use your restroom?"

"Ordinarily I would have directed her elsewhere, but she looked so forlorn and obviously in a hurry that I said, 'Sure,' and guided her to the first-floor ladies lounge."

The girl entered one of the booths. (I believe women have "booths" whereas men have "stalls.") She dropped part of her heavy rain gear on the floor.

A moment later two secretaries entered the restroom. Glancing under the booth divider, they saw a heavy pair of boots and men's trousers. They dashed out and into the lobby. "Barbara, Barbara, call a guard. There's a man in the ladies room!" Barbara explained the situation to them and gave assurance that their private inner-sanctum had not been violated.

✈ ✈ ✈

Not all the crackpots contacted Boeing by letter; some came in person and others resorted to the telephone. One woman stormed to the reception desk and demanded to see someone in the NSA. Asked to explain, she said that NSA was the National Security Administration. She declared that her body was wired and that she was receiving messages that the security people should know about. Barbara had to call a guard to persuade the woman to leave.

Phone calls were a headache. "I want to speak to Sally."

"Sally who?"

"I don't know her last name, but she sits by a window."

Again, "May I speak to George? I don't know his full name but he wears a gray suit."

✈ ✈ ✈

Names—A directory of Boeing employees would show last names for every latter of the alphabet—A to Z. Aaby, Aaker and Aalvik to Zylstra, Zysk and Zyskowski. At one time there was a chap whose name was Sexour.

Suzanna, a secretary, received a phone call. "Do you have a Sexour there at Plant Two?"

"No. We don't even get a coffee break," she replied.

✈ ✈ ✈

Paper Coming Up!—Bill Allen's afternoon *Seattle Times* was delivered to the front desk of the Administration Building. Barbara would place it on the stool in the elevator, then call Opal, Allen's secretary, on the third floor, that the paper was on the way and for her to pick it up from the elevator.

One day the paper disappeared. So from that day on, Barbara would put the paper aboard, then wait until the elevator had gone to the third floor and descended again, to make certain that the paper had been picked up.

She was standing thus one day, waiting for the elevator to descend, when T Wilson came up.

"Waiting for the elevator?" he asked.

Barbara nodded.

When the elevator door opened, T said, "You first."

"No thank you," Barbara replied.

"Weren't you waiting for the elevator?"

"Yes."

"Well, if you don't want to go up, why were you waiting for the elevator?"

"I'm an elevator watcher," Barbara stated as he walked away. This must have been before T became Chairman of the company.

✈ ✈ ✈ ✈ ✈

Alert Buyer—For the convenience of buyers who did not wish to have salesmen brought to their offices, a table with four chairs was provided in the lobby of the Administration Building.

Barbara had summoned a buyer (whose name shall not be used) to meet with the three salesmen who had asked to see him. The four took their seats at the table.

"The salesmen apparently had a lengthy sales pitch to make, as they took turns assailing the poor buyer," Barbara says. "The buyer was not only bored, he appeared to be getting increasingly drowsy. I watched the four from time to time between taking care of the normal flow of visitors.

"The buyer's head dropped lower and lower. His eyes would close, then suddenly open with a vacant look. Suddenly I saw him waiver and fall off his chair. He crashed to the floor and slid under a potted Norway pine, which decorated the lobby. Complete confusion took over. It was so funny that I broke up laughing and had to leave the desk temporarily. Throughout the day I kept breaking into laughter as I thought about the hilarious scene. People thought I had lost it."

Not that it was related to the lobby incident, but Barbara says that the full moon always brought out zany phone calls and visits from weird characters.

5

More Headquarters

Howard Hughes—tough to deal with

Give 'Em the Works—In the mid-1940s some veteran Boeing employees were approaching 30 years' service with the company. It was the practice to give employees a suitably engraved watch when they reached 25 years. What to do now that some were approaching 30 years?

A committee was formed to come up with the answer. A number of meetings were held, most suggestions being disapproved by John K., a particularly serious-minded individual.

Finally, a bit impatient with the lack of progress, a committee member suggested, "Why not just give them a watch case on the 25th anniversary and then on the 30th give them the works?"

John objected, "Now that's a silly idea. Who ever heard of a watch without works?"

He did have a point there.

✈ ✈ ✈ ✈ ✈

Overtime Pay—Like many executives, Bill Allen went to the office almost every Saturday. He found that much work could be accomplished freed from the interruptions of week-day activities.

The Allens had a married couple working for them. The man did the yard work and other outside chores, the wife worked inside as general maid. One weekend, the maid noting Allen's departure for the office, commiserated with Mrs. Allen, "My, it's a shame that Mr. Allen has to go to the office every Saturday!"

Then seeking something positive in the situation, she said, "But then think of all the overtime he makes!"

✈ ✈ ✈ ✈ ✈

Bill's T-Bird—Only on rare days did Bill Allen have lunch sent up to his office. Usually he came down to the Administration Building dining room and selected an empty chair at one of the tables. One day he sat down at the table where I was seated. After ordering, he said to me, "I see you are driving one of these new Thunderbirds. I guess you and Wellwood are getting too old for other things, so you go in for these sporty cars," he chided. Wellwood Beall, senior vice-president earlier had purchased one of the new Fords.

"Did you ever drive a T-Bird?" I asked. When Bill said "No," I proposed, "All right, let's trade cars

tonight. You drive my 'Bird' and I'll drive your Merc."
Agreed and keys exchanged. That Merc! Little power;
way over-steer!

The next morning when Allen called me to his
office to trade back keys, he said, "That was a mistake.
I shouldn't have driven your car home." I thought,
"Oh, oh. He's pranged it." Then he added, "The girls
(referring to his daughters) thought I had bought it."
A few days later he directed his assistant, Chuck
O'Brien, to arrange purchase of a Thunderbird. Deal
completed and car delivered. Bill drove the "Bird"
back and forth to work from that day on until his
retirement. The car, rebuilt twice, had well over
100,000 miles on it.

I don't think the daughters got to drive it much.

✈ ✈ ✈ ✈ ✈

Cock-eyed Racer—Ken Luplow was in charge
of the Boeing European office in Geneva, Switzerland.
He maintained contact with all Boeing's European
customers and acted as liaison between them and the
company headquarters in Seattle.

Among his other duties Luplow frequently escorted Boeing executives as they visited various airlines. Because of the comparatively short distances in
Europe, Ken usually drove the visitors as they made
their rounds of customer airlines.

On one such trip Ken was driving Mr. and Mrs.
Allen from Geneva to Rome. Descending a steep
mountain grade, Ken looked across the narrow valley
and saw a score of motorcycles approaching at high
speed. Obviously they were engaged in some type of
race. He moved to the edge of his lane and slowed to
20 miles an hour. On the racers came with engines
roaring.

Suddenly out of the pack a rider veered and hit Ken's Chevrolet head-on. Both Ken and Bill Allen, who was sitting in the front seat beside Ken, were horrified.

"That rider slid up the hood and right to the windshield in front of me," Allen related later. "We looked directly at each other, and I saw that his eyes were crossed. I thought the blow of hitting the car had crossed his eyes."

Police who were accompanying the racers stopped and assured Luplow he was not at fault. They also explained that the rider was naturally cross-eyed.

Seemed as though, with that handicap, he should not have been riding at high speed in a race.

✈ ✈ ✈ ✈ ✈

Where's Ben?—Ben Wheat held numerous positions during his years with the company. After a number of years at Wichita he was transferred to Seattle. Wheat left his family in Wichita temporarily and established a bridgehead at the Hyatt House near Sea-Tac airport. After two or three months he found it necessary to return to Wichita for several weeks. On his return he taxied to his old digs at the Hyatt House. He was greeted by a large reader-board facing Highway 99. It read, "Wheat, where have you been?"

✈ ✈ ✈ ✈ ✈

Typical Hughes—Wellwood Beall, Boeing senior vice-president in charge of sales, bore the brunt of many Hughes encounters. On one occasion Wellwood was in New York, just about to leave his hotel to return to Seattle, when Hughes called saying he had to talk to Wellwood personally and it was urgent that he do so as soon as possible. Beall cancelled his flight to Seattle and instead flew to Los Angeles.

Hughes, accompanied by a Hollywood starlet, met Beall and drove off to Venice, the amusement center on the beach. "Got to make a phone call, Wellwood. Take care of the girl. I'll catch up with you."

"We rode the merry-go-round and other rides for an hour or so," Beall related later. "I decided the young lady was getting hungry, so we found an eatery and had a bit of dinner. We dallied over coffee, and finally, after two hours, Howard showed up. As we drove in toward Los Angeles, Howard asked me where I was staying. I hadn't any intention of staying overnight, but I told him the Hollywood Roosevelt. Howard drove up in front of the hotel. I got out. A bellhop took my bag. Howard said, "'Nice seeing you' and drove off. I returned to Seattle the next day. Never did find out what he had in mind when he called me in New York."

✈ ✈ ✈ ✈ ✈

Expert Chef—Bill Allen gave a lawn party each year at his Highlands home for top management of the company. On occasion he also invited friends from the industry to participate. Chuck O'Brien, assistant to the president, recalls one such occasion quite vividly. "I was directed to pick up Dutch Kindelberger, president of North American Aviation, and take him to the Allens' for that evening's party," Chuck recalls. "On the way in from the airport Kindelberger asked me what was on the menu. When I told him steaks, he proceeded to give me a lecture on barbecuing steaks.

"'I'm generally known as one of the best barbecue chefs in southern California,' Kindelberger said. 'The secret is to use a meat thermometer, thrust it into the center of the steak, wait until the temperature reaches 125° to 130°, then serve it immediately.'

"Jim Boldt catered the lawn party," O'Brien continued. "Mr. Allen told us the exact time he wanted dinner served, so Boldt timed the steaks to be ready at that minute. But when dinner was announced, no one moved toward the tables. They were all too busy visiting and reminiscing. The steaks continued to cook on the grill, more than 100 of them. In desperation we took the steaks off and piled them into a couple of Boldt's electric warming ovens. Finally, 15 or 20 minutes later, the guests were all seated. Boldt took the steaks out, gave them a quick sear on the grill and served them.

"After the dinner Kindelberger called me aside. 'I'm glad you followed my advice about doing steaks,' he said. 'They were delicious, done just right. You know, when we were driving in from the airport, I was afraid you weren't paying attention.'"

✦ ✦ ✦ ✦ ✦

No Sale—Juan Trippe, president of Pan American World Airways, wanted to be the first to introduce jet travel to the American public. How he sought to buy the Boeing Dash-80 (prototype of the 707) was related by Bill Allen during a reminiscence session in his office shortly after he retired from active direction of the company.

"Did I ever tell you how Juan Trippe, of Pan American, wanted to get his hands on the Dash-80?" Bill asked.

"Trippe and I have laughed about it since then. We were in his office there at the top of the Chrysler Building negotiating contracts. Clyde Skeen was there.

We were in this room around a big table, and a number of people were taking part in the negotiations.

"Now and then Trippe would break the continuity of the meeting and try to get me to agree to sell them the Dash-80. At that time the Dash-80 was the only jet transport in the world other than the Comet. Trippe wanted to get the Dash-80, fly it all over the world, beat himself on the chest and say, 'Here is the only airplane. We're the leaders, you'll be riding with us in some of these soon.'

"We needed the airplane, of course, to carry out our test program. Trippe kept bringing the subject up. I said, 'Well, Juan, we are not going to sell you the Dash-80.' Skeen was sitting there, across the table, making marks on a tablet.

"In the elevator, after the meeting broke for dinner, I said to Clyde, 'What the hell were you scribbling over there across the table?' He said, 'I was keeping track of the number of times Trippe tried to buy the Dash-80. The tally was 17 times.'"

✈   ✈   ✈   ✈   ✈

Six Shooter—Fastest gun in the West might well have been applied to Bob Six, president of Continental Airlines. Six was a member of that exclusive group which practices "fast draw" electronically timed. Arms hanging loosely, right hand partially open and just opposite the gun butt in its holster, the contestant draws and fires on signal. No bullet spews from the .45; the shot is registered electronically. Speeds of the draw are usually registered in the hundredths of a second.

Six's prime interest, however, was Continental

Airlines, based in Denver. On one occasion Six brought his full board of directors to Seattle for one of its scheduled meetings and to visit the Boeing plant.

To entertain its guests, the company arranged a cocktail party to be held aboard a yacht cruising Lake Washington, with dinner downtown to follow. A well-stocked bar and a table of hors d'oeuvres had been set up in the main cabin of the yacht.

The boat had hardly left the dock when Six declared that he was going to hold his director meeting right then. His group repaired to the main cabin, and Six locked the doors. The Boeing hosts, including top officials of the company, paced the deck, looking with longing eyes at the refreshments locked in the cabin.

Eventually Six concluded his meeting, but by then it was time to dock and depart for the dinner site. Left behind was a choice cocktail assemblage.

✈   ✈   ✈   ✈   ✈

Whose Girl Friend?—Most financial houses have experts who concentrate on specific types of business. The aviation specialist of one of the larger Wall Street firms was a young lady, Muriel Seibert. Among her assignments was Boeing, whose operations she followed closely.

Muriel (her nickname was Micky) was on the phone frequently with Hal Haynes, vice-president finance, and Jim Prince, vice-president-secretary of the company. If both officers were unavailable, Muriel's calls were referred to me. We became good friends.

One day Haynes called me. "Your girl friend Muriel is coming to town. I'm tied up. How about you entertaining her? Take her to Canlis for dinner. See that she has transportation and anything else she needs."

My wife and I picked her up at the Olympic that evening. I sort of hastened checking her coat at the restaurant as it appeared to me to be imitation leopard.

A month or so later Haynes called me again. "Did you see the *Wall Street Journal* this morning? Our girl friend Muriel has just paid $440,000 for a seat on the stock exchange. First woman to buy a seat."

"Yes, I saw it," I replied. "And where do you get this 'our girl friend' business? She's still my girl friend."

Right then I decided that the leopard coat was for real.

✈ ✈ ✈ ✈ ✈

Hughes and Allen Clash—After the initial purchase of 707s by TWA under Howard Hughes, the airline made only one other small purchase of Boeing airplanes until after Hughes' death. Bill explained why in another discussion of Hughes and his idiosyncrasies.

"This is how our rapport terminated," Allen said. "I had continued to urge Howard to come up and fly the Dash-80, and he said he couldn't. 'I don't want to get on a commercial airline,' Howard said. 'All those people looking at me. I can tell they are making remarks.'

"So I said, 'I'll tell you what we'll do. It doesn't make sense for you not to see what you are buying. If you will give me notice, we'll bring the airplane down there and you can fly it for a day, but we will have to have it right back.'

"He said, 'That's fine. That's great.'

"We waited a couple of months, then he called and asked could we bring it down the next day. I said that was short notice, but we would see what we could do. I reminded him that it had to come right back.

"Well, it got down there, and at the conclusion of every day he would call and say, 'I'd like to have it just one more day.' This went on for a week. So I just called the crew on the phone and told them to bring the airplane home, period. Hughes must have had an underground or something because in less than five minutes he called me himself and said, 'I understand you've ordered the Dash-80 back.' I said, 'That's right.' He said, 'I just want it one more day.'

"I said 'You are not going to get it one more day. It has been down there for a week, and you are murdering our test program. She's coming home today.' He said, 'I've never had anybody talk to me that way before.' I said, 'Well, all right, there has to be a first time for everything. I don't want to be rude, but I'm determined on this. I've issued orders for the plane to come back.' He replied, 'I'll never buy another plane from the Boeing Company.' I said, 'That's too damn bad. I can't help it, but if that's the way it has to be, then that's it.' So that was the end of Allen and Hughes."

✈ ✈ ✈ ✈ ✈

Gee, Dad I . . . Roger Holman was one of a number of Boeing executives owning and flying their own airplanes. His was a Republic SeaBee, an amphibian. A boat-like fuselage permitted operation from water. Wheels retracted to the side of the fuselage were lowered for operation on land.

Holman frequently flew his plane from his lakefront home to the Renton airport. One day he took off with his young son as "co-pilot." After cruising about the area for some time and one or two water landings, Roger radioed the Renton tower that he was coming in to land.

Dutifully he entered the pattern and reported downwind. Then, turning to cross-wind and final, he concentrated on preparing for the landing. Ten degrees flaps, rpm back to 1,000, carb heat on. The numbers on the end of the runway grew larger.

"Dad, you . . ." "Don't interrupt me. I'm concentrating on landing," Roger admonished. "But Dad . . ." "Quiet!"

Roger flared for the touchdown when the wheels would gently kiss the runway. The touchdown was perfect—for a water landing. There was a clunk, clank and the screech of metal on concrete. Sparks flew. Finally the plane slewed to a stop.

"Gee, Dad, I was trying to tell you that you didn't have the landing gear down."

The next day Dave Nurse and his cohorts drew up a large chart of the Renton airport. But instead of the normal runway, they indicated, in its place, a long water canal. The drawing was presented to Holman for his use on future visits to Renton.

6

Renton

Hard deals and soft-hearted engineers

An Ostracized Duck—The second floor executive dining room at the Renton plant looks out on a four-sided court. A small reflection pool and various plantings, including several 4- or 5-foot evergreen trees in tubs, complement the ambiance.

One day diners noticed that a duck had dropped into the court and was placidly swimming about on the pond. In a few days it was further discovered that the duck was building a nest in one of the trees beside the pond.

The more learned of the engineering executives watching the operation pointed out that it was most unusual for a duck to build a nest in a tree and even more so when it was discovered that the hen duck was laying eggs. Those hard-headed, deep-thought engineers became an adoption agency for the duck and her potential family. Extra nesting material was made available. Food was supplied on a daily basis.

There was considerable speculation relative to the duck's unusual situation. Normally a drake stays with a hen through her egg laying and hatching period. Perhaps this was an unwed mother-to-be, hiding her shame in this isolated spot. Perhaps she had been banished by the flock.

Before long tiny quacks were heard from the nest, and six fluffy heads could be seen. Deep concern on the part of the engineers and other executives in the dining room! How were the ducklings to get down from their tree-nest to the pond where they would have to learn to swim?

Structure engineers went to work, overseen by a project engineer. A gently sloping ramp was designed and the drawings turned over to manufacturing for production. Then, with the mother duck away, the ramp, with its skid-proof walkway, was installed. In no time the ducklings were going back and forth on the ramp from nest to pond and back as though it were a normal procedure in duckdom.

Then a new worry. What was to happen when the ducklings became older? Could their mother induce them to fly up out of the courtyard? Could she take her family back to the arms of the flock, or would she be rejected?

Phyllis Birge, a secretary, and her husband solved the problem. They had a farm near Elma, and on it was a good-sized pond, ideal for ducks. One evening when the mother duck had settled her brood down for the night, the Birges stealthily approached the nest, gently captured the duck family and transplanted it to their farm where a duckhouse had been provided beside the pond. Presumably mother and children lived happily ever after, with a rare story to tell visiting ducks.

✈ ✈ ✈ ✈ ✈

The Great Alligator Hunt—Rumors were rife that an unusual large shape had been seen in the waters of Lake Washington, near the Boeing Renton plant. George Smith seized on the situation to promote the great alligator hunt.

George declared that what people were seeing was alligators. He said they, as small 6-inch animals, had doubtless been sold to children as pets and later had been flushed into the sewers by parents squeamish about the reptiles. He averred that the alligators had found their way to the warm waters being discharged into the lake by the Shuffelton steam plant and had grown to several feet in length.

"Best time to see them is just after dark, when they come out to feed in the lake," George told credulous listeners. Alligator hunt expeditions were arranged. For several nights, boats, their searchlights sweeping the lake waters, could be seen plying back and forth near the steam plant. No alligators were sighted. George maintained they were scared off by too many boats. Interest in alligator hunting ultimately waned.

Although years have passed since the alligator hunt, there are still people who aver they have seen a large mysterious shape in the lake. Some believe that the sighters may be partially right, that what they are seeing is an extra-large sturgeon which somehow got into the lake. It is a fact that sturgeon are taken readily in the Columbia River at the southern border of the State of Washington. It is possible, but only remotely likely, that a sturgeon somehow migrated to Puget Sound and thence to Lake Washington.

✈ ✈ ✈ ✈ ✈

Tex Wins a Bet—Willingness to assume a risk, if soundly convinced of its position, has marked Boeing at several key situations in its history. Claire Egtvedt took a substantial risk in the case of the B-17; Bill Allen risked 15 million on the Dash-80, prototype of the 707.

Another Boeing official willing to take a gamble was Tex Bouillioun, president of the Boeing Airplane Company. TWA was about to make a decision whether to purchase the Boeing 767 or Airbus Industries' A-310.

A principal selling feature of the 767 was (and is) its fuel economy which Boeing maintained was superior to the A-310. Fuel costs are a major factor to an airline, as Bouillioun well knew.

Confident of his position, but nevertheless aware of the risk involved, Tex made his pitch. He offered to bet that the 767 fuel consumption would prove to be well below that of the A-310. If not, Boeing would reduce the price of the airplanes substantially. If lower, TWA would pay the first agreed price.

Back at the plant Tex asked Joe Sutter and Ken Holtby, chief honchos on the 767 program, to sign a memo confirming their prognostication on fuel consumption. He mentioned dire consequences if they were not correct.

After a certain period of operation of the two aircraft, an analysis of the performance figures proved Boeing correct. Boeing got the contract, and at the original price.

Tex had filled a four-card flush, but in this case he knew where the cards lay.

✈ ✈ ✈ ✈ ✈

Charley to the Rescue—Again, the principal of this incident must remain unidentified, other than that he was a supervisor in the Renton plant. Out with the boys one night, he had taken aboard a bit too much and was picked up for DWI. He was taken to jail and his bail set at $250.

He used his one permitted phone call to ring Charley Moffet, getting Charley out of bed at 2:30 in the morning. He asked Charley to come down and bail him out.

Fortunately, Charley happened to have cash on hand and appeared at the jail with the necessary bail money. The sergeant on duty said, "Mr. X ain't going nowhere right now. We're using him in a line-up." Charley looked in and saw the most woebegone, dejected individual he had beheld for a long time. The poor chap was in the middle of a line-up of assorted scroungy characters.

When finally freed on the bond Charley had brought, the ex-jailbird said, "My god, I'm glad to see you Charley; it was terrible. They've had me in five different line-ups, and I've been positively identified twice as robbing a 7-11 store and once as having committed rape!"

✈ ✈ ✈ ✈ ✈

Small Change—When Boeing sold a 727 commercial jet liner to the Jordanian airline, Jordan's King Hussein, with a retinue, came to Seattle to take delivery of the aircraft. The king is a pilot in his own right and thus particularly interested in the plane his country was acquiring.

Dave Peterson, customer relations representative for the commercial airplane operations of the company, was among a group of Boeing officials who went to Vancouver, BC, to meet the king and his party and escort them to Seattle.

Included in the royal party was the king's helicopter pilot, Captain Zaza, who apparently also was acting as personal aide to the king. He drew Peterson aside and said, "We need a bit of cash in American currency. Could you arrange to cash a couple of checks for us?"

"Imagine my surprise when he gave me a traveler's check for $25,000, a cashier's check for the same amount and a third check on a London bank for $50,000," Peterson relates. "When we reached Seattle, it was after banking hours. Bill Allen got on the phone with some of his banker friends. They pointed out that they didn't have that kind of loose change lying about and that all their vaults were on time locks and couldn't be opened until Monday morning.

"Finally a company official contacted a couple of friends who dealt primarily in liquid funds, and he was able to cash one of the checks. Then we found a bank in the Burien area whose vaults were not on a time set. The president agreed to meet us and cash the second of the $25,000 checks.

"There we were with $50,000 in cash, mostly 10, 20 and 50-dollar bills. We put all the money into a cardboard box and took it to the hotel where the king's party occupied most of two floors. We took the money to the room of Captain Zaza and said, 'Well, we were able to cash two of your checks. The money is in this box.'

"'Oh, put it in the closet over there,'" he casually directed.

"We cashed the remaining $50,000 when the banks opened the next morning." The Jordanians paid cash for everything, including refueling of the plane on the return trip, hence the need for substantial amounts of currency.

✈ ✈ ✈ ✈ ✈

Mystery Trip—Tex Bouillioun, though only recently retired, has already become established as a legendary character. His wheeling-dealing style, while somewhat disconcerting to a few people, nevertheless led to phenomenal success of the Boeing Airplane Company during his tenure as president of that organization.

My first association with Tex, who came from the Wichita plant, was when we both were assigned to a management training program at the University of Washington. While most of us spent our evenings studying our program assignments, Tex found more interesting things to do in downtown Seattle. During his absence one evening we removed all the furniture from his room. Tex returned about one in the morning to his bare digs. Unperturbed, he immediately left to return downtown. To our surprise, he showed up at an early morning session fully prepared with the day's assignment.

✈ ✈ ✈

During establishment of the Minuteman program, there was great competition in Wyoming, Montana and the two Dakotas to have installation sites selected in their areas. Following selection of one site near Cheyenne, Wyoming, the community arranged an elaborate "appreciation banquet." Both senators, the governor, various mayors and other dignitaries were present. Tex had been delegated to represent Boeing. Called on for a few remarks, he outlined briefly the Minuteman program and then concluded, "Both my wife and I are having a delightful time on this, our second visit to Cheyenne. We were here before. It was on our honeymoon and we had a delightful time on that visit also."

On another occasion Tex was the central character of a James Bond type intrigue of far-reaching consequences. At this time Tex had become president of the Boeing Airplane Company. A mysterious caller asked Tex to come alone to the Olympic Hotel and come to a specific room. There he met a man of alien mien. The man said he knew of possible sale of airplanes to Roumania, but that it would have to be done his way. Tex agreed.

Tex was then instructed to go alone to Zurich, Switzerland. There he was instructed to leave all identification behind and to board a certain private jet. The flight plan and clearance indicated the flight was going to Athens and then Africa. Instead the plane landed at a remote field in Roumania. Slightly bewildered, but ever the gambler, Tex was met by two police who escorted him to a hotel. There he was assigned to a suite. He sat there for two days, meals and other amenities served at his wish.

"Finally on the third day I was escorted to a conference room," Tex relates. "There I was advised that Roumania would like to buy a Boeing commercial transport aircraft and a Vertol helicopter.

"I told them I could work their problem on airplanes but would have to check on helicopters, and would they please tell me what they wanted to do with the helicopter? They explained that it was for President Cocescu of Roumania in case he had to leave the country.

"Things were risky, I knew, since I was not sure if I was meeting with Roumanians or the KGB. I agreed to check on the helicopter if they would let me call out of the country and tell Boeing where I was. The phone had not worked the first two days I was there, but it worked fine when I returned to my room."

It was during this trip that Tex met the Chinese ambassador to Roumania. He advised Tex that the People's Republic of China wanted to buy Boeing airplanes. While it became quite involved and necessitated several trips to China, both Roumania and the People's Republic of China eventually bought Boeing aircraft.

Guess one could say that Tex filled an inside straight on that particular deal.

✈ ✈ ✈ ✈ ✈

Repeat Question Please—The session was being held in the board room of the Mitsubishi company in Tokyo. Leading the Boeing representative team was Dean Thornton, then head of the 767 jet transport project. Terms of a subcontract were being discussed, and the give and take was at times heated. The group was seated around a huge oak conference table.

At one point Thornton disagreed vehemently with a point being made by the Japanese. To emphasize his point, he brought his fist down sharply on the table as he declared a very positive "No."

Just as his fist banged the table, one of Japan's numerous earthquakes hit the Tokyo area. The building shook and there was the crash of glass from broken windows. The quake registered somewhere between five and six on the Richter scale. When the tremors had ceased and the excitement subsided, the business session resumed. Mr. Tojo, president of Mitsubishi, who was presiding, turned to Thornton and said, "Mr. Thornton, would you like to reconsider your answer?"

✈ ✈ ✈ ✈ ✈

One if by Land—In the early stages of introduction of the Boeing 707 and the Douglas DC-8, competition was unusually keen. This was particularly true with both companies having sales teams in Ireland seeking the Aer Lingus contract. The airline carried on extended consideration of the claims of each company, even though Ireland was distraught by the death of the current pope and anxious to learn the name of his successor.

The Boeing sales team, wanting to learn how they stood in the competition, called the Aer Lingus people repeatedly for a status report. They were told, "Don't call us, we'll let you know when we make a decision."

After three or four more days of waiting, the Boeing men could not restrain their anxiety. Again they called the top negotiator at Aer Lingus. Somewhat testily he said, "Look out your hotel window. You can clearly see our office building. Now keep an eye on the chimney. It will be black smoke if it's Douglas and white smoke if it's Boeing."

Must have been white smoke, as Boeing got the contract. And white smoke signalled burning of the final ballots at the Vatican and the election of a new pope.

7

Engineering

*Even austere slip-stick artists provide breaks
in the day's routine*

Repairs on a Mesa—Ingenuity is and always has been the trademark of Boeing engineers. Pan American World Airways and Trans-World Airlines were the first customers for Boeing's new four-engine 307 Stratoliner. The company had no service organization at that time, so Dick Rouzie, upcoming young engineer, was sent out to work with TWA during final check of the aircraft's enroute operation.

On a flight from Kansas City to the West Coast, the plane was at 18,000 feet and over the Rocky Mountains when two engines cut out due to icing. Otis Bryan, the pilot, immediately turned back to the east toward the assurance of more level ground. The 307 was maintaining altitude on two engines, but when it lost a third, descent had to be started. They were over a cloud layer when, through a brief hole, Rouzie saw cows and knew they were down to no more than 1,500 feet above ground.

Breaking into the clear, the pilot and Rouzie saw a flat mesa directly ahead with arroyos at each end. They slipped to a wheels-up landing on soft ground and slid some 300 yards. The lower baggage doors came open and scooped up dirt, filling the compartment as the plane skidded on its belly.

Rouzie and the flight crew went to work. In a nearby small town they managed to obtain a 5,000-pound jack. Railroad ties were brought in. The plane was jacked and placed on a crib of ties. In a few days four new engines and propellers were brought from Kansas City and mounted on the aircraft. Rouzie jury-rigged broken flap assemblies.

While the work was going on, Bill Westmoreland, TWA public relations man, came to the scene and busily rubbed dirt on the TWA insignia so it wouldn't show should reporters appear on the scene. With the repair work completed and with minimum load, the plane was flown off the mesa and to Kansas City for general overhaul. Gold star for Rouzie.

✈ ✈ ✈ ✈ ✈

Late to Work—Frank Terdina, assistant project engineer on the B-52 program, was a workaholic and expected the same of those working with him. Lysle Wood, chief engineer at that time, had just named Bill Cook as chief aerodynamist.

Terdina complained to Cook that while he and his men were working overtime on Saturdays, none of the aerodynamists were coming in to help them. T Wilson and Vaughn Blumenthal, assistants under Cook, were directed to give Terdina some relief. Rather than buck the problem down the line, the two decided to come in themselves on Saturday.

They arrived before 8 o'clock and sat around griping while they waited for Terdina. Finally at 8:30 they obtained time cards, punched in, wrote their names on the cards and added, "We're here, where the hell are you?" They then left the cards on Terdina's desk.

At 10:30 he called the two to his office. "I found your cards with their message," Terdina said. "I also noted that they were not addressed to me. So I took them up and left them on Lysle Wood's desk. As I came out of the boss's office, I locked the door, so there is no use your trying to recover those cards.

He neglected to tell them that he had found Wood's office locked and had merely chucked the cards in a wastebasket.

✈ ✈ ✈ ✈ ✈

Engineers Relax—The Staggering Stags was a rollicking group comprised largely of Boeing engineers with a few individuals from other operations. It existed in the late 1930s and up to the mid-1940s. The purpose: To provide relief from work tensions with an occasional two-day bash at some remote site. Today it would be called a "retreat." Favored points of visit were Big Four Inn and Lake Quinault Lodge.

Memorable was one of the trips to Lake Quinault. A bus was chartered, as usual, and a supply of peanuts and beer put on board to ease the strain of travel. With testing of the beer, a peanut war broke out and goobers filled the air. At a point somewhere below

Olympia, on an isolated stretch of highway, there was a general demand for a relief stop. There, lined up beside the road, the long line appeared like so many Mannequins Pis, that famed statue of a little boy relieving himself.

Late in the evening following dinner, several of the engineers sought amusement. They decided to measure the length of the emergency fire hose and found that it just reached nicely into the room of Roy Morse, who had retired early. Someone turned on the shut-off valve. The damage bill came to $90.

Among those gathered before the large walk-in fireplace were Glen Jones, George Synder, Amos Wood, Glen Dierst and Stan Leith, the latter two from plant protection.

"Do you remember last year when Kirik Pirogoff kept shooting firecrackers all evening and well into the night?" Don Patton asked. Just then Kirik appeared. In his hand was a huge red firecracker at least 12 inches long and 2 inches in diameter. He casually tossed the firecracker into the fireplace. A large davenport was overturned and numerous chairs upset in the mad scramble to escape the expected blast. Nothing happened. The firecracker was a dummy Kirik had made from cardboard and Christmas wrapping paper.

A subdued, tired and quiet group reboarded the bus the next afternoon for the return to Seattle. Just outside of Hoquiam a siren sounded, red lights flashed, and a car pulled in front of the bus. The bus pulled to the side of the road, and an officer with a large "Sheriff" badge entered.

"Which one of you is Charles Brewster?" When Charley raised his hand, the sheriff said, "Okay, come with me." Protesting and demanding to know why he was being taken in, Charley was driven to the jail, fingerprinted and placed in a cell. His fellow Stags followed to argue for his release. Finally Charley was freed.

"Damn it, Leith, you set that up," Charley challenged. Leith, who earlier had phoned his friend the sheriff, just grinned.

As engineering staffs grew, the Staggering Stags dissolved, or rather just expired. But there are still retirees who cherish their Staggering Stag certificate of membership.

✈ ✈ ✈ ✈ ✈

A Cooling Dip—Dick Rouzie and Bill Cook were among Boeing executives owning and flying their own planes—in this case joint ownership of an amphibious Widgeon. Accompanied by Dick Nelson and Wheeler Warren, they were returning from a fishing trip to the northern reaches of Vancouver Island.

Rouzie was flying and noting that they were getting low on fuel, decided to land at Pat Bay to refuel. He lowered the landing gear and trimmed for landing approach when he lost one engine. A moment later the second engine quit. Rouzie saw that he couldn't make it to the landing strip, so turned to land in the water. Without power he couldn't get the landing gear up.

As they landed (not the proper term for sitting down on water), the extended landing gear snubbed into the water. The plane flipped over and started to sink. Rouzie and Cook emerged, under water, through their respective windows, closely followed by Nelson and Wheeler. As they surfaced, an Indian, who had been fishing nearby, was already rowing over to pick them up. A rope was tied to the tail of the plane, and it was towed into shallow water. There it was determined that the major damage was to the nose. Rouzie dismissed the incident as "a slight pilot error."

Later Evan Nelson, company treasurer, was talking to Bill Allen. Having concern for four valuable engineers, he said, "Bill, can't you keep your people from getting into scrapes like this?" Allen replied, "Do you know any good way to slow them down?"

✈ ✈ ✈ ✈ ✈

Ker Boom!—Harassing new car owners was the particular delight of engineers in the early days when engineering was located on the second floor of the Administration Building at Plant One.

The Chrysler Company had just brought out its rather radical new automobile model, the Airflow. Tommy Enders was one of the first in Seattle to buy one of the new cars. With ownership pride he parked it in front of the Ad Building one day. His peers surreptitiously fastened a smoke bomb to the engine. When Enders turned the ignition key, smoke belched from the hood and a loud hissing noise followed. Enders emerged running—to the guffaws of his fellow engineers.

Lysle Wood, owner of a new Pontiac had, unfortunately, been away during the Enders episode. His car, parked on the street in front of the Ad Building, also received the bomb treatment with similar result.

Despite what some people think, engineers are human after all.

✈ ✈ ✈ ✈ ✈

T Wilson at times could be a bit of a curmudgeon

according to some of his associates. On this particular occasion the mood was amplified by a bad cold.

As Dean Thornton and others of his staff on the 767 program were making a detailed presentation, Wilson sat scowling and blowing his nose. He suddenly exclaimed in a rasping voice, "It's obvious you guys haven't done your homework. Now get the hell out of here until you can come back with a reasonable presentation."

A week or so later, after making very minor alterations in their presentation, the group returned to T's office. Obviously he had conquered his cold. He listened attentively through the complete presentation, then said, "Now you're on the right track. Go ahead."

✈ ✈ ✈ ✈ ✈

"Thar She Goes"—In the early stages of the Bomarc test program, as in practically all programs, problems were being experienced. On one scheduled test firing at Cape Canaveral, one problem after another arose and the actual firing was delayed repeatedly.

Finally in disgust one of the Boeing crew exclaimed, "Why don't we dig a hole in the sand, bury the thing, then set off a smoke bomb, point at the sky and yell 'There she goes'?"

✈ ✈ ✈ ✈ ✈

Whose Coat?—Jack Steiner had worked long hours almost to the time for him to catch a plane to Los Angeles. He dashed from his office, grabbed his topcoat from the rack at the head of the stairs in the engineering building. Another dash to the airport just in time to catch his flight. Boarding the plane, he handed his coat to the cabin attendant.

At Los Angeles Steiner was handed his coat as he departed. Outside the terminal, noting a rare Los Angeles coolness, he donned the coat only to discover that it was too large for him. The sleeves dangled beyond his hands, the shoulders were too wide. He returned to the airline counter to complain that he had been given the wrong coat. They would check.

He returned to Seattle carrying the maverick coat and bewailing the inefficiency of the airline. A couple of days later, departing his office, he noted a single coat on the rack. It looked strangely familiar. On it he found a note. "Will the so-and-so who took my coat put it back and take this one. It is far too small for me."

✈ ✈ ✈ ✈ ✈

A Pair of Pliers—Today's multiplicity of electrical and accoustical laboratories at Boeing's Seattle operations are a far cry from 1938 when the company had its first electrical lab. The equipment consisted of a pair of pliers, a screwdriver and a voltmeter. Further, the equipment did not belong to the company; it was the private property of Karl Martinez brought from his home shop.

Later Martinez was placed in charge of a fully-equipped accoustical-electrical laboratory after the necessary testing equipment had been purchased. In a soundproof room used in vibration tests of airplane parts, Martinez' equipment could set up vibrations varying from 18 to 6,000 cycles per second.

Wellwood Beall, then chief engineer, was interested in the vibration tests. He was placed in the test room and the oscillator-amplifier output brought down to 18 cycles per second. At that rate the human body gets into sync with the equipment. Beall was rather rotund, and assailed by the low frequency vibrations, his ample "belly" shook like a bowl of Jello, according to Martinez.

Boeing engineering ingenuity was once again demonstrated when a new insulation was required to protect high temperature wire in the Dynasoar. Martinez found it not in some company specializing in insulation but at the Coors brewery in Golden, Colorado. A specially developed ceramic material was used by the brewery to line its large vats. The ceramic with its high heat resistance proved perfect for the Dynasoar job.

✈ ✈ ✈ ✈ ✈

Boeing's Hidden Cave—Mention "the cave" to most Boeing people and only a few—a very few—will know what you are talking about.

As World War II neared a victorious end, management became concerned as to what direction the company should take when military production was completed. Following William E. Boeing's dictum, when he formed the company, "to leave no stone unturned," Ed Wells, chief engineer, selected a special group of engineers under Don Euler. They were isolated to a hidden uptown office-loft—"the cave." Their assignment was to dream up and design products of any type, other than aircraft, which the company might build and market after the war. It was an idyllic assignment for the engineering mind—"Let your imagination take full sway."

Some of the things the wheel-and-deal group came up with included:

A railroad coach with standard height vestibules, but with a lowered floor, reducing overall height by 2 feet and raising the center of gravity. A high-speed Spanish train uses this type of suspension. No doubt the design would have gone farther had the airplane not dictated demise of general railroad passenger traffic.

A kitchen cabinet with horizontal sliding doors (no more banging into open swinging doors).

A refrigerator with unique arrangement of storage areas.

An eggbeater, with pistol grip, adjustable for right- or left-handed persons.

A water metering valve, such as in a bathroom sink, adjustable with one hand.

A unit workshop. It consisted of bench, table and band saws, lathe, drill press, grinder, sander and vise. All the power tools retracted below the work surface.

A bicycle, shaft driven, rather than with a chain.

A bathroom-kitchen unit, 4 feet wide, 10 feet long and 8 feet high. One side of the unit comprised refrigerator, sink, four-burner range with oven, sliding door cabinet, and laundry unit below. On the opposite side of the unit were bathtub, toilet, lavatory and heater.

The complete unit could be taken in through the door of a house under construction. Simple hooking up of the utilities and the complete unit was in business.

Patents for the unit were sold to a private manufacturing company. A number of the units were installed in Alaskan housing projects.

Most unique was an automobile. Though it was

conceived and a mock-up constructed more than 40 years ago, it embodied many features found in today's cars and some which could well be added to today's designs. The machine had the inside passenger room of a Cadillac but the wheelbase and overall length of a Willys, a car comparable to today's Toyota. The bumper strip ran completely around the car for added protection, a feature recently adopted by a well-known French car. One could move from the rear to the front seat without leaving the car. The engine was in the rear to put added weight on the traction wheels.

Following design, a mobile mock-up was built, embodying everything but the engine which was not yet available. People could sit in the car and experience its advantage while being pushed around the loft floor by "engineer" power.

Extensive market research studies ultimately dictated that Boeing, like the shoemaker, should stick to its last and that aircraft and allied products should be its forte. That this ultimate decision was the correct one is proved by today's successes. But I sure would like to have an automobile cloned from that mock-up!

Oh, yes! Those engineers did indeed design "a better mouse trap." It threw the dead mouse some distance away and then reset itself, ready for the next intruder.

Final decisions made, the "cave" was closed down and the free-wheeling engineers reassigned to more mundane projects.

8

Plant Protection— Company CIA

The unique Stan Leith and his minions

Stan's "Computer"—If 10,000 men were placed on a stadium floor and you were asked to pick out the only one among them who was a cop, the law, you invariably would have pointed to Stan Leith.

Youthful helper of his moonshining relatives in North Carolina, center on a team which each evening played stooge to the Harlem Globe Trotters, and FBI agent. Such was the background of Stan before he became assistant and later head of the plant protection department of the Boeing Company. He had a staff of several score guards and firemen.

Crag-faced, raw-boned, large ears, gnarled knuckles, a rasping voice, more nerve than that accorded

government mules and finally an indescribable aura—
that was Stan. He had contacts everywhere from his
FBI days and a network of informants who kept him
well aware of activities throughout the Boeing organization.

Leith not only looked as one expected a detective
to look, he thought like one as well. Long before the
electronic computer came into general use, Stan's
brain functioned as a personal computer into which
he fed data for future recovery. Which leads to our
public relations power scooter. The scooter carried
three people on a cushioned seat in front. It was used
to take important visitors through the plant, a full
tour being too much of a walk for the average person.

One day I went to get the scooter. When I sought
to kick the starter arm, there was nothing there. I
lifted the seat to discover that the engine was missing.

The theft was duly reported to plant protection, a
new engine installed, and the matter forgotten.

Two months later a phone call came from Stan.
"This is Leith. I'm up town. What's the number of that
scooter engine of yourn that was stole?" Stan sometimes abused the subtleties of grammar. I'm sure it
was a put-on.

Given the number, Stan said, "Okay, I found the
fellow what stole it. He's in the hospital."

Later the details came out. A brief one-column, 2-
inch story on an inside page of the *Seattle Times* told
of a fire on a 24-foot cruiser on Lake Union, apparently started by malfunction of the boat's auxiliary
power plant. The article mentioned in passing that
the hospitalized, badly burned owner was a Boeing
employee.

Stan's "computer" went to work. Boeing employee.

Unusual for a boat that size to have an auxiliary power plant. What kind of engine runs it? He procured a search warrant, boarded the boat and identified our scooter engine hooked to a generator. The hapless employee, heavily bandaged, was served with papers charging theft of company property. He was later tried and found guilty. Employment terminated.

✈ ✈ ✈ ✈ ✈

Shakedown—The *Boeing Magazine*, a slick-paper monthly distributed to customers, libraries, key military, and the media was also given to company employees. On publication day stacks of the magazines were placed at the various exit gates where the guards passed them out as they carried on their routine inspection of employees' lunch buckets and parcels at shift change.

At the main exit on East Marginal Way, the guard was passing out magazines when the stack fell over. The slick-cover magazines slithered along the walk. The guard closed the gate temporarily while he gathered up and re-stacked the magazines.

Meanwhile a growing line of exiting employees backed up behind the closed gate. Someone whispered, "It's a shakedown! Pass the word." With the magazines restored, the guard opened the gate and the crowd filed through. Behind them on the ground where they had stood was a collection of micrometers, boxed pencils, calipers and such other small articles as could be hidden in one's pockets.

Not to sniff at Boeing employees. Very likely a shakedown of the thousands of employees flowing out of department stores and offices uptown would disclose similar cases of occasional light-fingered "borrowings."

✈ ✈ ✈ ✈ ✈

God Will Get You!—Industrial diamonds are used extensively in many phases of manufacturing, particularly in the aircraft industry where measurements are to the 10-thousandths of an inch and only the finest cutting tools—in this case diamonds—can achieve the degree of accuracy required. Thus it was that Boeing used extensive quantities of industrial diamonds. While not as expensive, nor of such high grade as the cut stones which grace the fingers of brides, nevertheless a handful of industrial diamonds has substantial value.

For some time it was noted that diamonds were disappearing from one of the shops. By some mysterious operation of his instinct and deductive cunning. Stan Leith centered on the leader of an in-plant religious noon-time singing group as a strong suspect. With search warrant in hand, Leith went to the small house occupied by several cult members. The suspect leader was at home. When Stan served the warrant and indicated he was going to start a search, the minister, in great indignation declared, "As God is my judge, Mr. Leith, I wouldn't steal the company's diamonds." All this time he was edging slowly toward the wall, one hand behind his back. Just as he reached the wall, Leith grabbed his arm, pulled it forward and disclosed a heavy pouch of diamonds. The minister apparently had intended to drop the booty into a hole in the wall.

Later when found guilty in a court trial and sentence had been pronounced, the minister arose at his counsel table and pointing a trembling and accusing finger at Leith declared, "God will get you for this!"

✈ ✈ ✈ ✈ ✈

$40 Room!—The congressional Un-American Activities Committee was a special concern of J. Edgar Hoover. One of the committee's meetings was scheduled for Los Angeles, and Leith had been invited to attend.

Arriving at the swank downtown hotel where the meeting was being held, Stan found himself in the registration line behind a young hand-holding couple, obviously just married.

He couldn't help hearing the conversation. "The rate is $40, take it or leave it," the looking-down-his-nose clerk stated. (This was in the late '40s when $40 was a high price for a hotel room.)

The bridegroom protested, "But when I made the reservation, they said the rate would be $20. Gee, we can't afford $40."

"Well, it's $40. You're holding up the line."

The young couple turned to walk away, tears in the girl's eyes.

"Just a minute," Stan said, stopping the couple. "You kids wait over there." Then he stepped to the counter. "My name is Leith. I'm here with Mr. Hoover and his committee."

"Oh yes, Mr. Leith," the clerk fawned. "Your reservation was made. We have an extra nice room for you, and the committee has a special rate of only $20."

"All right, Buster. I'll tell you what you do. You give my room to these two kids, and at that special rate. Now I'm going to the bar, and in five minutes I want you to have another room for me—same rate."

Before the time was up, Stan was summoned

from the bar and escorted to his room. A few minutes later there was a knock at the door. He opened it to find a bellhop holding aloft a tray on which rested a bottle of Hudson Bay Best Procurable scotch.

"Now what?" Stan demanded. "The hotel is so hard up it's pushing liquor?"

"Mr. Leith, all us bellhops chipped in to buy this bottle for you. We've been waiting a long time for someone to take that smart-ass clerk."

✈ ✈ ✈ ✈ ✈

Leith From Washington—Stan had a thing about hotels and delighted in outwitting them or showing up the arrogance of certain employees as in the case of the young newlyweds.

Once, arriving in Chicago, Stan called several hotels, only to be told there were no rooms available due to a large national convention.

He proceeded to the largest of the hotels, brusquely passed the people waiting in the check-in line and declared to the busy clerk, "Leith from Washington. I assume you've already registered me. I'd like to go right to my room. If the White House calls, I'll take it."

The harried clerk, thinking there must have been a slip-up, assigned Leith a room. (Hotels always hold back a few spots for VIPs and other emergencies, just as railroads and airlines do.) A bellhop sped Stan and his luggage to a choice room.

Now analyze the situation. He said he was from Washington. He didn't say "DC" and he was from Washington, the state. He didn't say he had a reservation, though he left room for that assumption. He didn't say he expected a call from the White House, only that if the White House called, he would take it. No deception there. Even you and I would take a call

from the White House. But none of us has the nerve to
set the stage as Stan had.

✈ ✈ ✈ ✈ ✈

Hallelujah Chorus—Among the potpourri of
workers hired by Boeing during the war days was a
group of religious fanatics—members of one of those
peculiar-name sects that spring up from time to time.
They were good workers, but irked their fellow employees with their insistence on singing hymns during the lunch break.

The problem was bucked up the line through
various levels until it reached Leith in plant protection. He solved the problem by arranging for a large
covered van to be parked on the apron outside the
plant work area. There the religious group could have
its noontime song-sings. With Machiavellian glee
Leith directed that the truck be parked next to the
Administration Building, right under my window.
Stan, a great friend to have!

✈ ✈ ✈ ✈ ✈

Stan and Willie Relax—Occasionally, as sur-
cease from his duties, Leith, with his wife Wilhelmina,
would take off for a few days in Las Vegas. On these
trips he took with him his unique facility for meeting
any situation head-on.

The Leiths checked in at one of the posh Strip
hotels. Stan proceeded to look up his numerous friends
among the security personnel of the various inns and
casinos. Willie, armed with rolls of quarters, attacked
the slot machines.

On the morning of their second day Willie was
taking a shower. She backed into the enclosure glass
door which, inexplicably, shattered, cutting her derri-

ere rather severely. After application of his first aid skills, Stan took Willie to the hospital, where several stitches were required to close the wound.

Back at the hotel, Stan called the manager, explaining what had happened and asked what the hotel proposed to do about Willie's doctor and hospital bills. "Shower doors are supposed to be shatterproof," Stan added.

"It's not our responsibility, Mr. Leith. Your wife must have done something unusual to break the door. We can't do anything about it."

"Okay," Stan said, "that's your position."

Leaving Willie sitting gingerly on a pillow, Stan drove to a downtown photography store.

"I want a dozen used flash bulbs," he told the clerk.

"Used flash bulbs?" the clerk asked incredulously.

"You heard right," Stan answered.

At the hotel he proceeded to strew the used bulbs around the room, then summoned a cleaning woman. She surveyed the broken shower door, picked up the broken glass and the flash bulbs and retreated. Apparently she reported the strange situation to management. In a few minutes the manager was on the phone.

"What's with all these flash bulbs in your room, Mr. Leith?" he asked.

"No problem," Stan answered. "You've established your position. When I get back to Seattle, our attorney will want evidence of the accident when we file suit. I was just taking pictures of the shattered door."

"Now, Mr. Leith, we don't want trouble. I'll be right up to talk to you.

The upshot was that the hotel not only paid

Willie's medical bills, it also picked up their room and accrued charges and their air fare back to Seattle.

✈ ✈ ✈ ✈ ✈

Hot Tip—Because of his FBI experience and his membership in the national police organization "Footprints," Stan had a wide acquaintanceship among the security forces of the various casinos in Las Vegas. On one of his periodic visits to the gambling center, a security friend casually mentioned that a race track betting coup was being devised by a couple of local big time gamblers. He thought Stan might be interested because the horse's name was "Gate Pass."

The gamblers had bought and trained this horse which displayed phenomenal speed. They had entered him in three races at California tracks with stern instructions to the jockey to finish out of the money in each instance. They were now planning to ship the horse to a Midwest track to complete the coup.

A couple of weeks later Stan was checking into a Kansas City hotel. The bell captain was reading a Racing Form. "Got a hot one?" Stan asked. "I like No. 7 in the 8th," the bellman replied, pointing out the horse in the racing chart. Glancing at the race indicated, Stan was surprised to see the name "Gate Pass" as an entry.

"I'd take a flyer on that No. 6 horse, Gate Pass, if I was betting," Stan said. "No way, man," the bellman exclaimed. "Look at the odds, 35 to one. No. 6! He's a dog! Never finished in the money in any of his races."

The next evening when he returned to the hotel, Stan was astonished at the greeting he received. "Man, we arranged to move you into a suite. We left a bottle of scotch and a bottle of bourbon in the cooler. Didn't know which you liked. Dinner is on the house." "What's the deal?" Stan asked.

"We talked it over. Us bellhops and the front desk clerk. We figure you the man we hear about. The man who fix races. You the man all right. We pools a hundred bucks and put it on No. 6 nose. He win. We win big. Anything you wants, let us know. You got anything else coming up soon?"

Stan checked out the next day. Didn't want to spoil his reputation.

✈ ✈ ✈ ✈ ✈

Phenomenon—Sitting in the DC-6 bound for Washington, DC, Leith appraised his immediate traveling companions. This stemmed from long practice as an FBI agent and now head of plant protection and security at the Boeing Company.

Beside him in the window seat, he catalogued a presumed cleric. The man wore a conservative black suit and his collar was reversed. Further, he addressed Stan as "brother." From behind him the fumes of alcohol marked the middle-aged man as having spent too much time at the airport bar.

In the aisle seat opposite Stan sat a good-looking young lady, whose age he appraised as 28 or 30. Her solidly filled, low-cut sweater accentuated her charms.

After completing his survey, Stan sat relaxed for a few minutes. Suddenly he became alert to what he detected, from the corner of his eyes, as a definite movement within the sweater across the aisle. Up and down, up and down, on the left side. More movement, side to side. This time on the right. No novice, Stan had seen many a performer who could twirl tassels suspended from both appurtenances, but never acting singly, nor in opposite directions.

He became aware that he was not alone in close attention to the phenomenon. The drunk was leaning on the back of Stan's seat enthralled. Sensing the directed interest of the other two, the cleric had turned and was staring across the aisle in what for him must have been a new experience.

The tableau persisted for a minute or more when the young lady became aware of the undivided attention being accorded her. She regarded her audience for a moment, smiled softly, turned and leaned into the aisle toward the three oglers. Slowly, very slowly, she reached into her sweater, searched about a bit, then pulled out—a pet mouse!

"I'll be damned if it didn't have a small rhinestone collar," Stan declared later. "After petting it a bit, she gave us another smile and replaced the mouse where it had come from. Apparently it had free run of the territory."

✈ ✈ ✈ ✈ ✈

Problem Gals—A continuing problem to plant protection during the war years was the ladies of the night who hired on for production work but spent most of their time lining up customers for their more lucrative evening hours. They were ousted as fast as they could be discovered.

Stan had an unerring eye for such trollops. In final assembly one day he spotted a woman he recognized. "Get that broad out of the plant at once," he directed.

A couple of hours later he was surprised to see the woman in a phone booth near the Boeing cafeteria.

Outside the booth several men were lined up. It was obvious that the enterprising dame had established a bridgehead and was signing up business.

Pushing aside the man at the head of the line, Stan said, "All right, sister. You are fired and you are under arrest."

"You can't fire me," she replied. "I just quit. And you can't arrest me. This isn't company property. This phone booth belongs to the telephone company. And they lease the land it's sitting on from Boeing!"

Done in by a doxie! For one of the very few times in his life, Stan had to admit defeat.

✈ ✈ ✈ ✈ ✈

Stan, Babysitter—No matter where he went, lady luck or her twin sister, lady fate, seemed to seek out Stan Leith. Again an east-bound airplane found Stan on board. He had an aisle seat in the first row aft of the lavatory.

Stan watched a young mother approach, baby in arms. She tried to open the lavatory door with one hand, the other arm cradling the baby. She decided she and the baby were not going to manage an entry.

Astute solution to the problem. She turned to Stan and said, "Would you mind holding him for a few moments?" at the same time placing the bundle in Stan's lap.

Two or three minutes passed. Suddenly Stan became aware of a warm sensation on his leg. Another minute and the mother reappeared. "Lady, your package leaks," Stan said as he passed over the baby.

On arrival in Chicago, Stan quickly donned his topcoat and buttoned it tight. He made his sodden way to a taxi and at the hotel send his suit out for a dry-cleaning.

✈ ✈ ✈ ✈ ✈

Strawman—The story is apocryphal and ascribed to various manufacturing plants in a number of cities. Nevertheless there is a considerable body of opinion that it actually did originate here in Seattle, more specifically at Boeing. For that reason, and for the benefit of the three or four who are not familiar with it, the story is set forth here.

Gate 18 off East Marginal Way is the principal entrance to the Boeing manufacturing complex at Plant Two. It also marks the crossing from the plant area to Boeing Field with its parking lots, auxiliary buildings and the flight test center. As a consequence Gate 18 sees a steady traffic throughout the day of persons going between work stations or to the parking lots.

One day several people were being checked through the gate, including a man pushing a wheelbarrow filled with straw.

"What have we got here?" the guard asked.

"Just some straw going across to the field."

The man was passed, and with the green light proceeded across East Marginal Way.

In the succeeding weeks the man with his barrow of straw made two more crossings. Having become a bit suspicious, the guard each time made a thorough search of the load of straw, but found nothing. He even inspected the bottom side of the wheelbarrow. Twice more the same thing happened.

Two weeks later the guard, on a Saturday-off day, happened to be in a tavern on Fourth Avenue South when the man of the wheelbarrows came in.

"Come on over and have a beer," the guard said. "Look, we are both off duty and anything you tell me I'll just forget. You've been getting away with something. What the hell is it?"

"That's easy. Wheelbarrows. And thanks for the beer."

✈ ✈ ✈ ✈ ✈

"All we wanted was . . ." In his younger days, well before joining Boeing, Leith was a deep sea diver assigned to the FBI office in Washington, DC.

In its routine of surveillance of the Washington scene, the bureau had strong reason for observing closely the activities of a certain alien. An agent was assigned to follow his every movement and to determine with what particular groups he was associating.

The tailing agent observed his target boarding a private cruiser which sailed off down the Potomac. Impossible to follow—all the agent could do was await return of the boat. When it finally appeared, his quarry was not aboard.

Detailed check was made of all possible landing points on the river and of residents along the waterway. Finally one couple reported having heard shots and a splash in the river. The spot was located as closely as possible.

A tug was chartered and Stan assigned to make dives in the area. After two days of searching the muddy bottom of the river, Stan located a body. A wooden platform was swung overboard and lowered into the water. Stan rolled the body onto the platform and signalled for it to be hoisted.

Brought to the surface and swung aboard the tug, the body was identified as the missing alien, even though it was covered with soft-shell crabs—the type considered a delicacy in the East.

His work completed, Stan directed the tug captain to mark the exact spot on a grid chart, then went below to change back into civilian clothes. When he returned topside to the deck, Stan was surprised to find the platform and its cargo missing and the crane which had lifted it, swung back overside.

"What goes on here," he demanded. "Who ordered that platform lowered back into the water?"

"Well, gee," one of the deckhands confessed, "We just wanted to get us some more crabs."

✈ ✈ ✈ ✈ ✈

Leprechauns Are Real—Stan Leith's one passion—outside of work—was boating and his 48-foot cruiser "Leprechaun." As is obvious, he carried his Irish heritage over to the name of his boat and his hobby. Leprechauns and trolls are related. Some maintain that leprechauns were originally trolls, but were banished from the strict Scandinavian mores because of their frivolous nature. Ireland, to which they fled, gave full rein to their blithe spirits. Fully appreciative of their pixy nature, Stan had a number of the little characters, both at home and aboard the cruiser named for them.

He had installed one of the little fellows—he called him "First Mate"—on a ledge between the helm and the binnacle. Then, with landlubbers aboard, he would surreptitiously put the craft on autopilot, abandon the wheel, and announce to his guests that "First Mate" was steering the craft. The more gullible believed him, it is said.

Cruising one summer in Canadian waters, Stan

put in at Pender Harbor, up the east coast of Vancouver Island. One other boat was tied up at the slip. In his usual outgoing manner, Stan greeted the skipper, who merely grunted and turned his back.

Shortly the wife came across the slip and apologized for her husband's demeanor. "He's very upset. Our engine is dead and we've been here for two days, while the rest of our cruising party has gone on ahead. My husband can't find the trouble, and we're trying to get a mechanic up from Nanaimo."

After an hour or two Stan took a couple of beers and went over where the distraught skipper sat in the cockpit of his boat.

Evidently the wife had rebuked her husband, for he was a bit more amiable. With the beer well sampled, Stan inquired, "Mind if I look around—your layout looks like mine."

"Won't do any good, what I need is a good engine mechanic."

Stan entered the forward cabin, checking various items. Behind the control cabinet, he removed a backing panel. There on the bus-bar which distributed power to various outlets, he saw a loose connection, hardly visible in the wire maze. He re-connected it.

Back topside he said, "I've got a little fellow aboard who is good on engines. I'll get him to have a check."

He returned with "First Mate" whom he took into the forward cabin.

"Let's have another beer while he's checking. He'll signal if he finds anything."

After a bit of small talk Stan exclaimed, "You've got it? Good! Little fellow says he found the trouble. Go in and try your engine."

Tapping his head and a nod to his wife to signal his skepticism, the man went in, pressed the starter button, and the engine roared into action.

The next morning Stan was listening on the shortwave radio when he heard the skipper, now under way, calling his cruising companions. "We're under way. Wait for us in Bute Inlet."

"Great! How did you fix your problem?"

"Well, you see it was this way. Ah, hell, it's a long explanation."

I know this is all true because I personally have seen "First Mate" take over and handle the boat.

9

Manufacturing

Doxies "assist" war effort

Unique Yardstick—Al Heiland personifies opportunity at Boeing. Starting as a beginner mechanic at 35 cents an hour, he was corporate director of management compensation at the time of his retirement.

In the early days, Heiland's boss was Claude Hill, one of the first Boeing employees. Heiland complained one day that there wasn't a yardstick in the entire company and that he needed one to lay out and have lumber cut for a storage shed he was working on.

Hill gave him a slat of hardwood and told Al to have it finished, painted white and marked off in inches, and he would have his yardstick. Al followed the various steps down to the final marking. One inch, two inches, etc., on to 35 and a final 36 at the end of the stick.

With his new tool Al completed the layout and had the lumber cut to his measurements. But when assembled, nothing fit! After considerable head scratching and cross accusations, it was discovered that in marking his stick, Al had somehow missed a number, jumping from 29 to 31—the only 35-inch yardstick in existence.

✈ ✈ ✈ ✈ ✈

Thanks, Navy!—While recruitment of enough workers to meet wartime requirements was difficult, Boeing did not exactly appreciate the recruits provided indirectly by the Navy. It began several hundred miles away in Ketchikan, Alaska. There a hard-headed and unsympathetic Navy type decided to rid the community of vice. Some 40 or 50 filles de joie were rounded up and unceremoniously herded aboard a boat headed for Seattle. Imbued with patriotism—hadn't they already given their best for the Navy?—the girls signed on with Boeing as factory workers immediately on their arrival in Seattle.

Plant Protection and the ever-alert Stan Leith soon discovered that the girls were contributing little to production. They were spending most of their time lining up business for their more lucrative off-shift evening hours.

Out! Terminated!

✈ ✈ ✈ ✈ ✈

"Ouch! My Hair!"—"While we had tough bosses and we worked hard, there was a certain amount of horseplay in those earlier days," Al Heiland recalls. "It was standard practice to nail down the lunch bucket of a new employee, or rub the inside of the handle with limburger cheese. A couple of the fellows had a Ford magneto which they would crank up and then touch some unsuspecting individual who was working on a metal jig. It would give a mild jolt and the sparks would fly.

"George Stenhouse was general foreman of the body shop where we were building fuselages for, I think, the 40B. Anyhow, George crept under the jig to inspect the bottom of the fuselage, just as a mechanic was drilling a rivet hole from above. The drill came through the metal, barely missing George's face, but entangling his hair. The rapidly spinning drill pulled out large chunks of hair before George's yell stopped the drill operator."

✈   ✈   ✈   ✈   ✈

Photogs Are Photogs—As he progressed through various positions in the plant, Heiland occasionally took part in labor negotiations. In one instance little progress was being made. As a break, Al invited the union representatives for a ride in his motorboat. Negotiations at that time were not as formal as today. After motoring out to the middle of Lake Washington, Al shut off the motor and said, "Look, guys, let's see if we can't work this out." There, rocking gently on the water, they did and returned to shore with an agreement.

I had several arguments with Al in trying to get raises approved for the photographers in our department. (They won't believe this.) Al had one classification for all photographers. I maintained that ours, spending many hours on photo flights, or shooting executives and prominent visitors, should be in a special category. Al argued, "Look, a photographer has a camera, he has film in it, he looks into a finder, sees what he wants to shoot and presses the shutter release. What difference does it make if he is shooting an assembly jig in the factory or an airplane? Besides, riding around in airplanes should be more fun than working in the factory."

I think Al would have relegated Steichen or Karsh to the hourly payroll. Eventually, public relations photographers were given special consideration. It must have been after Al retired.

✈ ✈ ✈ ✈ ✈

Boeing Does the Impossible—Oh, sure, it's easy enough to lose a pair of pliers, a peen hammer or a set of drawings. It happened at Boeing; may still be occurring. But lose a completed passenger airplane fuselage or a Pratt and Whitney engine? Impossible! On the other hand, Boeing often declared that it could do the impossible.

The company had received a limited order for 10 of the 307 Stratoliners. Manufacturing and assembly of the parts into a finished aircraft took place at Plant One. When work on the fuselages was completed, it was discovered that only nine were lined up to receive their empennages and undercarriages. A recheck showed that sufficient parts for 10 had been manufactured and gone through the various stages of assembly.

It hardly seemed a case of an employee pilfering something he could take out under his coat. Finally a maintenance man happened to become curious about a large tarp-covered object in a seldom-used warehouse area. Sure enough, the missing fuselage assembly! How it got there no one could explain.

Pratt and Whitney engines for a large order of military aircraft were shipped from Hartford, Connecticut, to Seattle by boat via the Panama Canal. Each engine was enclosed in a substantial crate, annotated in stencil to show that P and W and Air Force representatives certified that the crate contained one P and W engine. Manifests of the shipments were mailed to Seattle and checked against the individual crates as received at the plant.

Rather than returning the empty crates to Pratt and Whitney, they were removed to a general storage area outside the plant and made available to employees at $2 each. They made excellent playhouses, doghouses and had other utilitarian uses.

When one particular shipment was checked, it was short one engine. Telegrams, getting hotter as the argument progressed, went back and forth between Seattle and Hartford. Pratt and Whitney insisted their manifest was correct. Boeing maintained that the shipment was short one engine.

In the meantime, an employee brought his truck to work so that he could pick up a couple of the low-price crates. He managed to manhandle one of the crates onto his truck but found it difficult to move the second. He called on a friend to help him.

"How did you get the first one on?" the friend asked.

"I sort of rolled and joggled it on," the man replied.

"Well, if you did it once, two of us should be able to do it easily."

After considerable straining, the friend said, "That thing is just too damn heavy for an empty crate. Let's see what's in it." Off came the lid. "Jeeze, an engine! We better report this to the boss."

Red-faced officials confessed to Pratt and Whitney that their manifest was correct.

Can't lose a fuselage or an engine? Ha!

✈ ✈ ✈ ✈ ✈

Charm School—Chick Pitts, factory manager of the Boeing Wichita, Kansas plant, was self-consciously aware that he did not have the advanced education of some of his peers, according to T Wilson. In order to improve, Chick decided to learn a new word each day. He worked very hard at it and read a great deal, Wilson says. Whenever Chick encountered an unfamiliar word, he wrote it on his calendar and made it a point to use the word two or three times during the day. Aware of Chick's project, fellow workers made book on what the "word of the day" might be. Winner took the pot.

As another step in his self-betterment program, Chick enrolled in a management course. Its objectives were to improve communications with fellow workers, get their views, and indirectly induce them to certain actions in the belief that they themselves had conceived the desired results. In brief, its philosophy was "Don't tell a person to do something, lead him to make the desired decision." Skeptics in some quarters referred to the program as "charm school."

One day Chick took his assistant, Ernie Ochel, onto the balcony overlooking the final assembly area of the plant. Leading Ernie to the railing, Chick pointed to a large machine below and said, "Ernie, don't you think it would be advisable to move that machine down there across the aisle beside that other machine? It would expedite the flow of material."

"Naw," Ernie replied. "We've studied it, but it

would cost more to make the move than it would save."

"Ernie," Pitts persisted, "it would make for a more efficient operation and in the long run would pay off. We ought to look beyond the immediate situation."

Again Ernie objected. Pitts tried two or three more times, each time following closely the script for communication. Each time Ernie became more obdurate in his objection.

With the last positive "No" from Ochel, Pitts took off his hat, slammed it on the balcony railing and exclaimed, "Goddamn it, Ernie, move that machine!"

"There went the charm school," Wilson says.

✈ ✈ ✈ ✈ ✈

Divinia's Fordilac—Lowell Divinia, assistant to Earl Schaffer, Boeing vice-president and general manager of the Wichita operation, was of serious mien and stolid appearance. He also owned and drove the only Fordilac automobile in the U.S.

The Fordilac was a Model A Ford coupe in which Divinia had installed a Cadillac V-8 engine. It was his delight to pull up at a stoplight beside some youth in his chopped and blown hotrod.

With a look of disdain at the Ford, the youth would speed off when the light turned green, Divinia would let loose the 250 horsepower of the Cadillac, lay down rubber and leave a chagrined and bewildered youth behind.

✈ ✈ ✈ ✈ ✈

Top Secret—Designing, building and flight testing of the B-29 Superfortress was one of the prime secret projects of World War II.

At Plant Two the first XB-29 was being assembled. The work went on in a production bay screened off by canvas. A special pass was required to enter the area. Plant visitors, even top military brass, were detoured around the B-29 bay.

One day a letter addressed to Boeing found its way to our office. It was from a 12-year-old grade school lad in Laramie, Wyoming. It read: "Dear Boeing. Will you please send me pictures and all the details on the B-29? All I know about it is . . ." and he proceeded to give wing span, gross weight, power plant and other details which were top secret.

The letter was turned over to the Air Force representative at the plant. Never did find out where the lad got his information. We didn't send him any pictures.

✈ ✈ ✈ ✈ ✈

Bos Aids Boeing—That the placid, dumb cow, genus bos, could make significant contribution to the production of Boeing airplanes may seem farfetched; nevertheless, it has happened.

Production of printed circuit cards involved a process of transferring circuit drawings to sensitized copper plates. One of the steps required exhausting the air from a plastic bag. Available laboratory vacuum pumps failed to do the job. The problem was solved by Ramon Lubovich, who had kept a herd of milk cows before coming to work for Boeing. He was well-versed in the high vacuum capacity of the mechanical milking machine. Such a machine was adapted to the circuit-card problem. Result: Better and faster production.

Next problem: Removal of stubborn airplane bolts

up to 3/4-inch diameter. A stockyard stunner, with the knockout punch of Jack Dempsey, was borrowed from the stockyard industry. In its original application it was used to stun cattle as they followed their destiny to slaughter.

In slightly modified form the inexpensive stunners were provided to Boeing field teams working on the B-52. One blow and the most stubborn bolt was dislodged. Credit another plus to the ubiquitous cow. After all, a relationship to the aerospace industry does exist. Remember the cow that jumped over the moon?

✈ ✈ ✈ ✈ ✈

Free Assembly—Like many Boeing workmen, he had a home workshop, an extension of his daily work interest. A part of his garage was assigned to the project, and various equipment had been accumulated. His final need was for a bench lathe.

Now there were at least five ways he could obtain the desired piece of equipment. He could rent it, borrow it, receive it as a gift, buy it or steal it at work. He opted for the last. Over a period of months he requisitioned a part here, another there. As each part came into his possession, he covered it with heavy grease and dropped it out a window into the Duwamish River at the rear of the Plant Two machine shops. Then on off days or after working hours, he retrieved the greased object from the water and added it to his slowly-taking-form lathe.

Unknown to the miscreant, Stan Leith and his plant protection guards, learned of the nefarious plan. As each piece of equipment was dropped into the river and later recovered, Stan knew of the action and the particular part being eliminated from Boeing stores. Patiently Stan waited until the last item had been purloined and assembled into the now-completed lathe.

Then, with search warrant, he recovered the company property. Why not move in earlier? That way they would only have had parts. By waiting, they recovered a machine, assembled for free.

✈ ✈ ✈ ✈ ✈

Great Ad!—The ad was a stopper. Exceptional in concept and execution. The five major components of a B-17 Flying Fortress would be suspended in juxtaposition from overhead cranes in one of the bays of Plant Two. The purpose was to demonstrate Boeing's simplified method of building bombers whereby the major sections were completed separately and only joined as a completed airplane at the last minute before going out the factory door. The method was in sharp contrast to the "assembly line" technique practiced at Willow Run and elsewhere.

At the peak of production Boeing was turning out a B-17 at the rate of one an hour on the first and second shifts. The shortened third shift was devoted to maintenance and "pick-up."

Bob Richie, New York photographer, was given the assignment of producing the photo. Bob surveyed the factory bay and decided that to properly light the area, he would have to place at least 200 flashbulbs. Nearly a day was given to placing the bulbs and connecting them electrically to a single switch which Bob would punch when everything was in place and camera ready.

Came the momentous day. Cranes brought the

sections into place. Camera was set up on a high platform. Bob took one final check, then started to climb the ladder to the photo platform. At the top he reached to set the camera lens opening when there was a blinding flash. He had inadvertently pressed the switch and 200 flashbulbs went off!

Back to the salt mines. A crew was brought back in and the laborious job of replacing all the flashbulbs was started. The next day, with Bob very cautiously handling the flash switch, the picture was made, and eventually the striking ad appeared in a number of the national media. Got very high reader ratings.

✈ ✈ ✈ ✈ ✈

A Miracle!—Weekly top management meetings, presided over by President Bill Allen, were standard procedure. At one weekly meeting Bill Rutledge, representing manufacturing, painted an extremely gloomy picture of the situation in his area. In fact, he declared that unless drastic steps were taken, the company faced a definite crisis.

The next week at the customary meeting, Rutledge was all smiles and carefree. Noting the demeanor which was in sharp contrast to that of the week before, Allen said, "Rutledge, last week you took 10 minutes to tell us in detail that dire fate faced the company. You look happy today. What happened?

Rutledge grew an embarrassing red and then said, "Bill, it was a miracle."

10

The Military

Which sometimes took its job—and itself—too seriously

Colonel to Colonel—It is only rarely that the occasion, the circumstances and the personnel combine to create the perfect situation for a most apropos story. Such occurred on the day during World War II when Boeing was given an "E" award for "Excellence of Production." The military urged the company to make the most of the event.

All employees were dismissed from work to gather on the apron in front of Plant Two. There a speaker's platform was erected. A colonel flew in from his desk command in Washington, DC, to make the presentation and to give a talk intended to inspire the workers to even greater effort. He droned on interminably, no doubt setting production back rather than ahead.

Observing proper protocol, the company arranged

a small dinner for the colonel that evening. Among the limited number of guests was Colonel Chevalier, vice-president of McGraw Hill, New York publishing house, who happened to be in Seattle.

Following dinner, the Air Force colonel was called on for a few remarks. Again he went on to the point of boring all those assembled. When he finally finished, Colonel Chevalier was asked to end the evening with a final few words.

"I really haven't much to say," Chevalier began. "However, listening to the colonel this afternoon and again this evening reminds me, for some reason, of a weekend house party at an English country manor. After dinner, the guests withdrew to the game room and bridge tables were set up. Sir Ashley-Hampton drew as his playing partner Lady Chumley. She played very poorly, and when, after several hands, she trumped Ashley-Hampton's ace, he threw down his cards in disgust and exclaimed, 'You silly ass, why don't you learn how to play bridge?'

"In high dudgeon she went to the host and declared, 'I want Ashley-Hampton to leave at once. Either he leaves or I go. He has insulted me deeply.'

"Insulted you? What did he do?

"'He called me a silly ass!'

"Why, Lady Chumley, think nothing of it," the host said, patting her arm. "Good heavens, I've been out of the Army for 20 years and they *still* call me colonel."

Chevalier's story broke up the party. The Washington colonel was not amused.

✈ ✈ ✈ ✈ ✈

Wartime Sillies—In retrospect, many of the fears, near panics and actions in the early days following the Japanese raid on Pearl Harbor appear, at best, foolish and in some respects downright stupid. Immediate bombing of West Coast cities, particularly Seattle with its Boeing plants, was rumored, though no bomber existed which could fly the Pacific to the U.S. mainland. Planes flying from Japanese carriers standing off the U.S. coast again would not have the necessary range.

As a war-time measure, East Marginal Way leading to the Boeing Plant Two was closed to all but Boeing traffic. Blackout curtains were installed in all office windows. These actions were taken at the direction of the military. The most cruel, of course, was the removal and internment of American citizens of Japanese ancestry.

Barrage balloons were brought in and placed in a large circle around the Boeing plant and around the Bremerton Navy Yard. They were raised at night to a height of some 2,000 feet, intended to discourage night bombing attack. Each morning, precisely at 8 o'clock, all the balloons were brought down to the ground in unison like the lowering of a curtain. It was a beautiful sight from the surrounding hills. Of course, enemy bombers would have had perfectly outlined targets, for at the center of one circle of balloons was the Boeing plant, in the other the Navy Yard.

Several million dollars were spent camouflaging Plant Two, including simulation of a complete town on the roof. With fear of bombing attacks continuing, the company was ordered to construct bomb shelters for all employees. These concrete boxlike structures, each accommodating perhaps 100 persons, were built on the west side of the airport, parallel to East Marginal Way. Shortly after completion of the shelter project, a test evacuation of the plant was ordered.

In preparation for the test, Stan Leith took a crew to make final inspection of the buildings. They were amazed to find that the shelters had obviously been used for love trysts, and further astonished to find families living in several. Migrants from the South, attracted by good wages, thought it right neighborly of Boeing to provide free living quarters for its recruited workers. They were ousted without ceremony.

The one and only evacuation test went off smoothly. A long thin column of men and women snaked from the plant, north on Marginal Way and thence to the assigned shelters. A pleasant interlude in the day's work; small contribution to the war effort.

✈ ✈ ✈ ✈ ✈

XB-52 Rollout—As rollout of the first XB-52 neared, the military moved in to handle security in connection with the event.

The XB was the first model of the eight-jet super-bomber, a radical advance in the military aviation field. It was built in Bay 1 at Plant Two. The tail was so high that it had to be hinged and folded over to get the plane out of the factory and into most military hangars.

Came the big day, or rather night. The military insisted the rollout must be at night. Further, that the plane should be completely covered so that none of its details could be seen. Several hundred yards of muslin were purchased for the cover-up. East Marginal Way was closed to all traffic. A company of infantry was brought in from Fort Lewis for guard duty. The rollout was set for 11 p.m.

Vern Manion was on hand with his camera to record the event. Assisting him, I took a flash gun and climbed high on a maintenance platform. Vern told me to shoot the flash when he signaled.

The factory doors slowly opened. A tug pulled the huge plane, ghost-like in its flapping draperies, out onto the apron. Vern gave the signal and I shot the flash, then started to back down the ladder from my perch. As I neared the bottom, I felt a bayonet at my rear, and one of the soldiers said, "You can't take no pictures!" I said, "I sure can't. This is a flash gun, not a camera." His commanding lieutenant finally was convinced that indeed I couldn't take pictures.

As a follow-up and an indication of the inanity of some military minds, Manion was required to send his undeveloped film to Washington for developing, printing and clearance. To take the film from the holders, Manion used the standard black light-proof bag, into which he placed the holder and his hands to remove the film. One of the security officers insisted on placing his hands in the bag with Vern's to assure that no hocus-pocus took place.

The plane was towed across Marginal Way to the field and backed into a revetment where the military insisted final work would have to be done. Further, first flight test would have to be at night.

As everyone in Seattle knows, 200- or 300-foot high hills are immediately to the east of Boeing Field. Houses along a principal street dot the hillsides. It would be impossible to build a revetment high enough to shield the B-52 from view. Too, no test pilot in his right mind would make a first flight at night, nor would any responsible executive order it.

We got in touch with our friend Colonel (later General) Arno Luehman, overall head of security review for the Air Force in the Pentagon. We explained the situation to him and asked him to come out and see for himself. The next day he flew in. We took him up on the hill and showed him all of Boeing Field and the plant below. He made a quick call to Washington. Presto, the silly restrictions were rescinded and sanity returned to the program. I wouldn't be surprised if Boeing still has several hundred yards of muslin on hand.

The B-52 is still in service well over 30 years after its introduction into the arsenal of the Strategic Air Command.

✈ ✈ ✈ ✈ ✈

A variety of Air Force Plant Representatives were stationed at Boeing over the years. Some were knowledgeable and efficient, some just average; only one or two were overbearing and arrogant. In the early war days, Ewen Dingwall, who later managed the Seattle World's Fair and still later the Seattle Center, was on the public relations staff. His office was on the first floor of the Administration Building, facing toward the curved driveway to the building entrance.

One day the current Air Force rep—and he qualified as one of the few on the negative list—came walking along the driveway. For some reason Dingwall's secretary, standing at the window, spontaneously expressed her regard for the colonel by placing her hands to her ears and wiggling her fingers.

Unfortunately, the colonel happened to look up at that moment and saw her. He stormed through the lobby and up to the office of P.G. Johnson, then Boeing president. He demanded that the secretary's boss be fired immediately. After calming the colonel and taking care of the business at hand, Johnson called

Harold Mansfield, head of public relations, and told him of the colonel's ultimatum. Mansfield pointed out that Dingwall wasn't even in his office and argued strenuously that Dingwall could hardly be held accountable for the actions of the scatter-brained secretary. Johnson finally compromised by agreeing that the girl be demoted and transferred. I don't know if Dingwall ever learned how close he came to being fired.

✈ ✈ ✈

Later the company inherited another negative Air Force plant rep. Not satisfied with the usual office in the DPC building, he demanded an office next to Bill Allen, who succeeded Johnson as president. Further, he insisted that the office be furnished with a pink rug.

With his departure to another assignment, sanity returned, and the new rep moved back into the usual quarters in the DPC building where his staff was located. Maintenance was left with a surplus pink rug. It finally wound up in our New York public relations office.

✈ ✈ ✈ ✈ ✈

Sergeant Meets General—The Paris Air Show, which alternates with the English Farnborough Show, is a prestigious affair in which many nations take part. Boeing started participating at Paris as far back as the mid-'50s.

At one of the earlier shows I was one of several Boeing representatives. Featured were aircraft from a number of nations. The Russians sent the TU-103, their newest passenger jet. They opened it to the public, and a long line of people was constantly waiting to go through the craft.

The United States was represented by the Boeing 707 Air Force II, one of the two identical Presidential planes. However, no one was permitted to enter the American plane.

After listening to comments about the restriction on the U.S. plane while the Russian plane was open to all, I looked up the Air Force public relations representative accompanying the Presidential plane and said, "Look, the Russians have their plane open to the public and the U.S. plane is off limits. The U.S., the Air Force and Boeing are being made to look ridiculous. How about getting in touch with Washington and seeing if something can't be done?"

Top public relations and security personnel in Washington were apprised of the situation directly through the long-range radio of the Presidential plane. After an apparent conference, word came through— "Let the public go through Air Force II."

Presidential planes are rather posh. Compartmentalized, with a special room for the President, a dining area, map and situation room, and an area for a limited number of media reps.

A large, burly Russian general, in his ankle-length overcoat, was one of the visitors. He was being escorted by a young sergeant attached to Air Force II. Scanning about, the Russian asked, "And vot is this airplane used for?"

"Troop transport, sir," the sergeant replied.

Right there I mentally awarded the sergeant a distinguished service medal.

✈   ✈   ✈   ✈   ✈

A Lot of Crab—The Air Force Association is an organization of civilians interested in national defense and a strong Air Force. The largest chapter in the country in the 1950s was located in Omaha, which is also the site of a major Air Force base and at that time a Stroz brewery. (Not to be confused with the present day Strohs brewery.) Mr. Stroz, president of the brewery company, was also head of the Omaha Air Force Association chapter and its most enthusiastic booster.

On occasion, the Air Force would fly key members of the Association to visit various defense plants. One such trip was set up for the Omaha chapter to visit Fairchild Air Force base in Spokane, and then on for a tour of the Boeing Seattle operations. Before the flight left Omaha, Mr. Stroz phoned us and asked if we could procure two 20-pound salmon and a dozen king crabs for him, as he wanted to bring them back to friends in Omaha.

We checked a local seafood wholesaler who said he could supply us without problem, but "that's an awful lot of king crab." A bit concerned after the wholesaler's declaration, I decided to check with Mr. Stroz. I managed to reach him at the Spokane air base BOQ.

"Mr. Stroz, we have the salmon for you. Are you sure you want a whole dozen king crabs?"

"Oh, yes," he replied. "Back in Omaha we are very fond of your crab. I guess you have another name for it. Dungeness, I believe."

Slight difference between a 4-foot king crab and a 16-inch Dungeness!

✈ ✈ ✈ ✈ ✈

A Tree for Omah—The request came through from General LeMay at Strategic Air Command headquarters in Omaha. "People back here haven't seen Christmas trees like you have out there in Washington. Could you supply us with one?" The problem was bucked down to public relations and in turn to Pete Bush. His only instructions: "Find the best tree you can and get it back to Omaha."

Pete checked first with company drivers. One who often passed through the Maple Valley area reported a beautiful tree, perhaps 100 feet tall, on a farm in the valley. Pete made a deal: $100 for the tree. He then had the tree cut, borrowed a cherry picker crane from Paccar to load it on a truck for delivery to Boeing Field.

Transportation to Omaha? No problem. A C-97 cargo plane, dubbed "The Shrimp Boat," flew regularly between Seattle and Hartford, Connecticut. From the east it returned with a load of Pratt and Whitney engines for installation in Boeing aircraft.

It got its name because on its empty flights east it frequently carried Alaska shrimp, Dungeness crab and Puget Sound salmon for Boeing employees stationed in the East and hungry for Pacific seafood.

Only a few feet had to be cut from the base of the tree in order to accommodate it to the 80-foot C-97 cabin length.

Delivered to Omaha and set up at the Air Force base, it was by far the largest and grandest Christmas tree ever to grace the State of Nebraska.

✈ ✈ ✈ ✈ ✈

New York Premiere—Among the many postwar motion picture flying epics was "Twelve O'clock High," with Boeing B-17 Flying Fortresses playing an important role in the production.

First night premiere of the picture was to be held in New York with stars of the picture and a host of other Hollywood representatives on hand.

Preceding the evening gala a special luncheon for the press and New York dignitaries was held in the Waldorf Astoria. Tex McCrary, husband of Jinx Falkenberg, and a radio and TV star in his own right, presided as master of ceremonies.

Joining Tex at the head table was a B-17 crew which had seen action in Europe and had flown in from its California base especially for the New York ceremony.

At the end of the meal Tex first introduced the crew and the more noted of the guests.

Then proceeding to a climax, he said, "And now I want you all to greet the feminine star of the picture, the beautiful Miss (and here I have to confess that I have forgotten her name) who is just entering the room. It seems appropriate that she be given proper military escort. Sergeant will you do the honors?" and he pointed to a bashful-looking, sandy haired youth of not more than 20.

The sergeant accepted the assignment with alacrity and hastened to the portals of the room where the young lady waited. She took his arm and they started for the dais.

"By the way, sergeant, what is your position on the plane?" Tex asked.

"Tail gunner, sir!"

The crowd roared and gave the sergeant a hand as he completed his mission.

✈ ✈ ✈ ✈ ✈

The Arrow—The method of naming and numbering Boeing aircraft had been of interest to both the

Engines on top of wing? They are as Tex Johnston rolls the Dash-80 over the Gold Cup races.

Realistic camouflage village of burlap and plasterboard-covered roof of Plant Two as a war-time measure.

More camouflage. Front of Plant Two with finished B-17s on apron at right.

Workers leaving bomb shelter after practice air raid alert. Women outnumber men workers.

Long rows of employees returning from their assigned air raid shelters, the concrete structures in the rear.

Rollout of the XB-52--at night, draped in muslin and troop-guarded, as ordered by military security.

124

First flight of the restored Boeing 100. Lou Wallick (in cockpit) and Bob Muckelstone, left, are co-owners. Orville Tosh, at right, did the restoration.

Shot on the first flight of the Dash-80, 707 prototype. Manion's color picture appeared as a center spread in *Life* Magazine, just three days later.

Vern Manion with the author.

The author in cockpit of replica of Boeing's first airplane, the B&W. Clayton Scott, former Boeing test pilot, who built the replica, in rear cockpit.

Models get hungry. A break in picture shooting in the Stratocruiser mock-up. Manion, photographer, confers with the author.

By Wingett, left, and Vern Manion in their flight gear are prepared for another aerial photo session.

Spectacular head-on shot of the B-47; finally made after Manion first forced the camera plane to abort.

This group of South African newsmen is typical of overseas press visitors to Boeing.

Club 21 celebration of Dash-80 delivery to the Smithsonian. Manion made this timed shot while one foot stood in a sink of chipped ice.

Tex Johnston, left, and Col. Guy Townsend, right, with Art Curran, center, prepared for another flight test of the XB-52.

Mt. Rainier is used so often as background for Boeing pictures, such as this of a B-52, that some people refer to the famed mountain as "Mt. Boeing."

Cockeyed B-52. With the B-52's nose pointed into a cross wind, the landing gear points straight down the runway. Picture by Vern Manion before Tex Johnston "chased" him with the big bomber.

Four famous Boeing bombers in stacked formation. Bottom to top: B-52, B-47, B-29 and B-17. One of most difficult shots they ever made, Manion and Wingett aver.

press and the public. At one period in the 1950s the Air Force was operating so many Boeing types, B-29, B-47, B-50 and B-52, that Pentagon wags would facetiously explain that the "B" actually stood for Boeing rather than bomber or bombardment.

Several officers once suggested to a serious minded Boeing official that the company's next aircraft be named the "Boeing Arrow." The Boeing man explained that the company already had names selected for future production. Officers disappointed.

✈ ✈ ✈ ✈ ✈

A General's Solution—Secrecy surrounding rollout of the first XB-52 has been explained, particularly the difficulty with picture taking. When security review in Washington finally decided to release a picture to the press, there was considerable discussion as to just which shot to release.

Brigadier General Sory Smith proposed that they release a phony photo in which a picture of one B-52 would be superimposed above and just touching the other. "That'll confuse the bastards," someone observed before a true portrait of the B-52 was selected and released to the media.

11

La Femme

Nylons, romances and caramels

How Romance Is Born—Kay Kelley, a gorgeous redhead, worked in our public relations department. She came from Minnesota, twelfth child in a Johnson family in a Scandinavian settlement where the name Johnson was predominant.

Curious as to how a Johnson became a Kelley, and to give authenticity to this book, I obtained Kelley's address recently and wrote her for an explanation.

"As to my maiden name of Kelley! Yes, my grandfather's original last name was Johnson and he was Swedish. When he came over from Sweden and settled in a small town in Minnesota, there were so many people by the names of Johnson, Nelson, Peterson, Olson and Carlson that all the mail got mixed up. So anyone who wanted to change his name could do so by paying $5 to the head councilman in charge of the town. Why my grandfather decided on the name of Kelley, spelled with an extra "e" is beyond me. He married my grandmother, who was Norwegian, so I am half Swede and half Norwegian with a name of Kelley."

I might add that she is married to an Italian.

Frank Elliot held forth in an office on the first floor of the Engineering Building, directly across the intervening alleyway from the public relations office. One day Frank called Kelley and asked for a date. Looking across the alleyway, he could see her at the phone. "By the way," he added, "Chuck O'Brien standing here wants to know if that cute brunette beside you would like to double date." She would. She did. They kept on dating. She became Mrs. Charles O'Brien. Score another for the romances which bloomed at Boeing.

✈ ✈ ✈ ✈ ✈

An Ignoble Retreat—For obvious reasons, the principals in this dramatic bit must remain anonymous.

Occasionally, in order that undivided attention be directed to solution of particular problems, the company arranged retreats at remote locations. One such retreat to a lodge on a distant lake included several men accompanied by two secretaries to record the proceedings.

Afternoon sessions were followed by an hour of relaxation, dinner and more work. Late one afternoon one of the two secretaries was in her room ironing a dress for the evening dinner. Just out of the shower, she stood stark naked as she ironed. Perhaps it was her normal approach to the tedious task. Unfortunately, she had left her hallway door slightly ajar.

The least liked male of the "retreaters" happened down the hallway, glanced in, pushed the door open and slapped the nude on her well-shaped bare behind.

With rage in her eyes and murder in her heart, she pulled loose the electric connection and started after the miscreant, waving the sizzling iron and threatening to brand him. He ran down the hall, iron-wielder on his heels, out the door and across the short span of lawn toward the lodge dock. While she paused at the lawn's edge, he continued to the end of the dock and into the water. Fortunately he could swim.

The young lady returned to her room, finished ironing and appeared well clothed and unruffled at dinner. She was only slightly daunted when applause greeted her entry.

✈ ✈ ✈ ✈ ✈

Out of Line—Orville Graves, original owner of Snoqualmie Falls Lodge, had to shut down his operation during World War II because of the shortage of restaurant supplies and rationed gasoline. He came to work at Boeing as so many did during the war. One of his duties was to escort new hires on a tour of the plant to acquaint them with the area in which they would be working.

Graves and Chuck O'Brien were good friends. Graves made it a habit to point out to Chuck any particularly good-looking girls who might be among the new hires or whom he might encounter in the plant.

"Whenever Ginny gets out of line," O'Brien says of his wife, formerly a secretary at Boeing, "I inform her that she was *not* one of the girls Graves pointed out to me!"

✈ ✈ ✈ ✈ ✈

Romance Blooms Again—Boeing is a great place for romance. Early on in World War II, the now-defunct *Look* magazine sent a crew to do a story on the contribution of women to the war effort. They selected a good-looking young teletype operator, Evelyn Kerr, as one of the featured persons for their story.

We in turn assigned a recently hired photographer, By Wingett, to assist the *Look* crew. By split his attention between the work at hand and the young teletype operator. They were married not too long after.

The *Look* people were intrigued with the development and took the young couple on a paid honeymoon with a consequent feature story in the magazine.

Now skip forward 12 or 15 years. The 727 was to be sent on a demonstration tour around the world, and a photographer was to accompany the flight. We always tried to equalize the assignments of the photographers among exciting and tedious tasks. Since Manion and Wingett had accumulated equal amounts of "sad time"—the photographers' term for dull assignments and night duty—I decided to have them match for the 727 world trip. The two came to my office. I flipped a coin. Wingett called "tails" and the coin showed heads. "Sorry, By, you lose. Manion, you are elected."

Only a few weeks later I received a phone call from my friend Ben Kociver, senior editor of *Look*.

"We are planning a feature story on all the major national parks in the West," he said. "We're looking for a personable young couple with two or three children. We'll take them on a six-weeks' tour, all expenses paid. Do you have any suggestions for such a couple?"

"Ben," I said, "remember about 15 years ago when you did a feature by taking a newly married couple, the Wingetts, on their honeymoon? Well, Wingett still works for this department. They now have three children six to 11 years old, and we will give him the time off if you want them."

So, while Manion got the trip around the world, Wingett and his family had a six weeks' holiday covering everything from Glacier Park to the Grand Canyon and winding up in Las Vegas. You may remember the feature story as it appeared in *Look*.

Too bad *Look* has folded. No telling what it might have done with By and Evelyn the third time around.

✈ ✈ ✈ ✈ ✈

A Pair of Nylons—War-time shortages were a serious problem in England and continued after the Germans had been defeated. When he learned that I was to visit England, my friend Maurice Smith, editor of the English magazines *Flying* and *Motor Car*, asked if I could possibly bring a couple of pairs of nylons for his wife Vivian, as none were available in England.

I picked up a dozen pair at New York's Saks and, at a nearby delicatessen, a box of various goodies which were not available in food-short England. Everyone deplaning in London seemed to be carrying a food package of substantial size. Just ahead of me in the customs line was the captain of our flight. He lifted an obviously very heavy, stoutly-corded box to the inspection table.

"And what is this?" the customs agent asked as he attempted to heft the box.

"It's a cake," the captain replied.

"Quite obviously it's a cake," the agent declared as he marked the package "cleared" for entry. He didn't ask what I had, just cleared the package.

Vivian was delighted with a half dozen pairs of the hose. I distributed the rest among other friends. However, when I reached the airport for my return, I found I still had a pair of the nylons left.

As a special service BOAC had ground attendants similar to flight attendants. The duty of these ground personnel was to assist passengers through departure red tape and generally keep them happy. A lass of some 18 years, with characteristic English pink cheeks, was assisting me.

With some hesitancy I said to her, "Look, I hope you won't think this impertinent, but I have a pair of nylon stockings left from some I brought for friends. I don't want to take them home with me. Would you like them?"

"I've never had a pair in my life," the girl whispered as she took the package. Then she started to cry. Gosh, I almost started crying too!

✈ ✈ ✈ ✈ ✈

Den Mother—Marge Blair was a surrogate den mother to headquarters. If one had business visitors coming from out of town, one called Marge. She arranged to have them met, made hotel reservations, etc. If you needed to entertain at dinner, call Marge and she made all the reservations and arrangements. Need a company car to take a guest uptown? Call Marge and she in turn would call Jim Luster. Jim was in charge of the headquarters building garage. He kept the cars clean, fueled and ready to go. Jim, highly popular with everyone, happened to be black. He and Marge had a close working relationship because of their respective duties.

If some minor glitch occurred, Marge would say in mock seriousness, "Jim, if you don't shape up, I'm going to give you a white eye!"

✈ ✈ ✈ ✈ ✈

Corny but True—Even Hollywood would have said, "Too corny. Besides, the Cinderella story has been told a dozen times." Corny or not, here are the facts.

During World War II, women comprised more than 50 percent of the Boeing work force. They did everything from driving rivets to running lathes. Among these feminine workers was Vickie, a beautiful young lady of 19 endowed with an unusual amount of patriotism. She worked as a wire harness assembler. In addition, she served three nights a week as a volunteer in the aircraft spotting headquarters. She gave blood at the blood bank; assisted at the Red Cross.

Because of her good looks and because she typified the contribution of women to the war effort, we frequently used Vickie as a model in publicity and advertising photography.

One of the experts hired to do advertising illustrations was Robert Yarnell Richie, noted New York photographer. His wife was the daughter of a prominent eastern industrialist. During one of the photography sessions, Vickie was used as a key model and, of course, was directed by Richie. Apparently he became enamored of the innocent young aircraft worker.

It was a surprise some months later when it was learned that Richie had divorced his wife and married our Vickie. Though she had never before been out of the State of Washington, she fit into New York life with amazing adaptability. They lived in an apartment on exclusive Murray Hill. She accompanied Richie on many of his worldwide assignments. Occasionally we would receive postcards from Texas, or Africa, or Saudi Arabia.

Before too long they were made happy by arrival of a daughter. Then, a few years ago, I got a phone call. "This is Vickie! Guess what! I'm back at Boeing. Bob fell in love with a secretary down in Texas and asked me for a divorce. We're still friends."

The daughter grew up to be as beautiful and charming as her mother.

A few months ago I was shocked to learn that Vickie had died, ending the Cinderella story of a girl from Seattle who had gone off with Prince Charming, become a sophisticated world traveler and, when the clock struck 12, returned to Seattle and her original surroundings, even a job with her old company.

Too corny for Hollywood. But true.

✈ ✈ ✈ ✈ ✈

No More Caramels—My secretary, Helena Munnell, was and still is beautiful with unusual light ash-gray hair. On a lunch break she had just tossed a caramel into her mouth and started up the stairs to the second floor when she met Mr. Allen coming down.

"Young lady," he said, stopping the startled girl on a landing. "Don't ever let anyone tell you to do anything to your hair. It's beautiful!"

"Thumk you very muth, Mither Allen," she said through caramel-clogged teeth.

"I was never so embarrassed in my life," she said on returning to the office. She had an aversion to caramels from that time on.

✈ ✈ ✈ ✈ ✈

Joe's Bar—Dora Hunter learned to be certain who was on the other end of the telephone line before giving a facetious answer. Dick Rouzie had rushed into Dora's office and declared he had to see Mr. Beall right away. "I told him Mr. Beall was on the phone," Dora recalls. "Instead of waiting, Mr. Rouzie said he would dash back to his office and call me right back.

"Soon the phone rang and, thinking it was Dick, I answered, 'Joe's Bar.' The voice on the other end said, 'Is Joe there?' But it wasn't Dick Rouzie! It was Mr. del Valle of Pan American Airways. Right then he became one of my favorite people, and I never again answered the phone that way."

12

Public Relations

A gorgeous nude and a million golf balls

Gorgeous Nude—The Boeing advertising agency. N.W. Ayer and Son, had developed a series of ad layouts featuring the interior of the Stratocruiser. The plane was a deluxe passenger transport featuring a lower deck lounge and main deck seats which converted to full size berths at night. It was a sensation when introduced in the early '50s.

One of the ads was to show a young mother tucking her little girl in bed in one of the luxury berths. It was decided to make the shots in Hollywood where a plethora of models were available. The interior of the plane could be simulated by those clever movie scene-makers.

First step was selection of models. A call went to

Central Casting requesting an audition of little girls, five to six years old. More than 30 mothers showed up, each shepherding a young hopeful who the mother was sure would be another Shirley Temple. We picked a cherubic little curly-headed blonde of five years. Another call to Central Casting brought a dozen young mother types. Decisions, decisions! Finally we selected one and with reluctance dismissed the rest.

Ah, Hollywood! The berth was simulated by a couple of sawhorses across which a plywood sheet was laid and on top of that a mattress. The proper linens were applied. The curved wall of the cabin had been duplicated by the studio carpenters. The berth, being a lower, had a window. As background, through the window, a cyclorama duplicated sky.

"How about some stars showing outside through the window? This is a night shot, you know," the agency man inquired.

"No problem," one of the grips said. He went backstage, punched a half-dozen holes in the cyc. Then he placed a spotlight behind the holes. Presto! Stars!

During a break in the shooting, our "mother" and the cherubic little girl were singing "Bell Bottom Trousers," and that little angel knew all the words of the bawdy version.

Later, during another break, I wandered into the photographer's lab. On the wall was a full color picture of a stunning nude, with a fox fur draped around her neck and covering strategic areas.

"Gad, that's a beautiful girl, well-built too. Some movie star?" I asked.

"Nope. Guess you didn't recognize her with her clothes on. She's the 'mother' you've got out there on your berth setup."

Somehow, in my mind, I just couldn't keep clothes on the girl during the rest of the shooting.

The pictures came out fine. You may have seen the resulting advertisement in the *Saturday Evening Post* or *Life* or other magazines.

✈ ✈ ✈ ✈ ✈

They're Only Dummies—Seattle's Northgate Shopping Mall was the first such operation in the United States. Consequently, its opening was marked with numerous ceremonies and community participation. Boeing was asked to contribute a number of special displays. Arranging them was assigned to Pete Bush.

Bush managed to assemble the top gun turret from a B-17, a number of airplane wheels, some other bits of body sections and a number of dummy bombs, highly realistic in appearance. All were loaded on a truck and driven to Northgate. There the truck crew, with Pete aboard, was directed to drive down the center of the covered mall to the assigned area close to a U.S. Army display.

The truck moved slowly down the mall, already crowded with early viewers. As the truck passed over a grating, the grid gave way and the truck tipped sideways. While the gun turret and other heavier equipment stayed on the truck, the bombs fell off and rolled in several directions. Water spurted from a broken water main under the grid. Women screamed, people rushed for the protection of stores, and general consternation reigned. Bush leaped from the truck and shouted, "No danger! Everything is all right. These are just dummy bombs!"

Sure that word of the disaster would soon reach

Boeing headquarters, Bush phoned me. "We've got a little problem out here at Northgate that you may hear about." Then with utter confidence he added, "We'll get it under control in half an hour or so."

To his rescue came several GIs from the Army exhibit. "Looks like you got a little trouble. We'll give you a hand."

One of the GIs got down in the hole and shut off the water. Another brought up a large earth-mover they were using in their display and lifted the Boeing truck from its hole. The break in the water main was welded, the dummy bombs rounded up and reloaded, the grid patched and repaired. Problem solved. Exhibit delivered. Mission accomplished. No casualties.

✈ ✈ ✈ ✈ ✈

Mansfield's "Bedburner"—Harold Mansfield, after giving up the public relations reins, wrote two highly successful books. The first, *Vision*, was the overall story of the birth, growth, trials and successes of the Boeing Company and the men who directed it. The second book, *Billion Dollar Battle*, was the story of the Boeing 727 and the gamble the company took with this radically different airplane. The book's title was awesome in its implications. Of course, today when Boeing annual sales and backlog run into the billions, the book title would hardly arch an eyebrow.

Vision was so successful that it went through two hardcover editions and was abridged in a paperback version. In production of the latter there occurred an unthinkable, a horrendously appalling error. Somehow in the binding process the first 32 pages were not the smooth-flowing prose of Mansfield. Instead they constituted the first 32 pages of *Limits of Love*, a "barnburner" or rather, one might say, a "bedburner," of raw passion in all its explicity.

Unfortunately, one of these early editions somehow got into the hands of Ben Wheat, a Boeing executive of sardonic humor. For months he delighted in ragging Mansfield about his pornographic prose.

If any of those first few books are still in existence, no doubt they are collectors' items.

✈ ✈ ✈ ✈ ✈

The Lamb Chop Caper—Some of the company's more routine advertising and publicity pictures were made in a mock-up section of the Stratocruiser. One evening (the mock-up was used by engineering and manufacturing during the day) a series of shots was being made showing the method of food service on the new passenger airplane. As a featured innovation, a passenger's food tray was placed on a folding table which let down from the back of the seat in front of him. It was a decided improvement over the lap pillow on which one precariously balanced his meal tray in earlier model aircraft.

Two dozen full-course dinners had been catered for use in the shooting. Lamb chops, petit pois, french fries, salad with tomatoes and radishes, and a raspberry tort—all planned for color effect. Shooting continued well into the evening. However, as models became tired and crew a bit testy, decision was made to knock off and continue the next evening.

Now in order that the food remain fresh-looking and appetizing under the hot floodlights and the extensive shooting, it was standard practice—a trick of the trade—to paint everything with castor oil. The oil gave the food highlights and at the same time preserved its freshness.

The set was saved intact for the next evening's shooting. The food trays were left in the galley of the mock-up. The castor oil would keep all fresh.

The next evening, when we prepared to resume shooting, we discovered to our dismay that little was left on several of our food trays save a few bones from the lamb chops. When I challenged plant protection to discover the culprit, it was sheepishly explained that two of the night guards had eaten several of the dinners, thinking that otherwise they would be discarded.

"Well, I want to talk to them," I demanded.

"They aren't coming in tonight. Both reported in sick. Bad cases of diarrhea."

✈ ✈ ✈ ✈ ✈

An Expensive Breakfast—With two or three hundred Boeing people traveling somewhere in the world on company business on any given day, it is not unusual that several of them should unexpectedly encounter each other. Therefore, it did not greatly surprise me, as I entered the dining room of the Drake Hotel in Chicago for breakfast, to be hailed from a corner table already occupied by several individuals.

I recognized Dave Peterson of customer relations. "Hey, public relations, come on over and join us," he greeted me. I knew one or two others of those at the table and was introduced to three engineers, a field service rep and a couple of sales types.

Midway through breakfast Peterson excused himself to make a phone call. Shortly after his return one of the engineers was paged and suggested that his companions go with him as the call was from Seattle and no doubt company business.

Engrossed in my eggs, I gradually became aware of the exodus of various individuals until I was alone.

The waiter brought over a check and laid it beside my plate. Glancing at it, I noted an assortment of entries and a total of just under $100. "What gives?" I asked. The waiter replied, "The man said to give it to his father, and he pointed at you."

In the lobby a grinning group awaited me. "Gotcha, public relations!" Peterson chortled.

How do you explain a $100 breakfast on an expense account?

✈ ✈ ✈ ✈ ✈

Wheels Up—Boeing editors and photographers were always trying for new "angles" in shooting pictures of aircraft. In the early stages of the B-52 eight-jet bomber program, they decided they would like an "underneath" head-on shot of the plane just as it left the runway and became airborne.

Shooting from the side of the runway did not produce the desired results. Unmanned, remote control cameras did no better. Obviously, to get the shot, the photographer would have to stand in the middle of the runway. The problem was taken up with Tex Johnston, test-pilot on the B-52 program.

"Okay, fellows, here's what we'll do," Tex proposed. "I'll take off at exactly the 4,500-foot mark. You be on the runway at the 5,500 mark, and I'll come directly overhead."

Pete Bush, no coward, along with Manion and his cameras, went to the middle of the runway at the designated mark. Tex started his roll, the B-52 coming faster and faster. As he had promised, Tex lifted the big ship off the runway at the 4,500-foot marker.

But, instead of then starting a climb, he simply raised the landing gear and passed just a few feet above the two on the runway. True to his dedication, Manion got the spectacular shot.

"The roar of those engines and the blast as they passed overhead actually shook our bodies and was deafening," Bush said later. Manion and Bush decided that Tex owed them one.

✈   ✈   ✈   ✈   ✈

Taxi Rodeo—It has long been my ambition to promote a world's championship taxi cab contest. With the consensus of Boeing friends I would select the top driver from, respectively, Paris, Rome, Mexico City and Tokyo.

My plan would be to place two of the drivers and their taxis at one end of a one-way street and the remaining two at the other end. A cannon would signal the start. Survivor would be the winner and champion.

✈   ✈   ✈   ✈   ✈

Gee, Thanks, Boss—Advertising was one of the several functions assigned to the public relations department. Working with our advertising agencies, we had to prepare an annual budget and present it to the board of directors for approval. One of the directors was Artemus Gates, New York financier and director of a number of companies, including Time-Life.

For several years we had used *Life* magazine as one of the media in which we placed ads. However, we eliminated *Life* this particular year, as its rates had become so high that they over-balanced our budget. I presented the proposed budget to the board and then withdrew to await the verdict. Word came down that the budget was approved.

Late in the afternoon when the board had adjourned, I received a summons to Bill Allen's office. He greeted me, "Artemus here is wondering how come you eliminated *Life* from your proposed budget. Well, I have to step down the hall for a few minutes, so I'll leave you two alone."

Gee, thanks, boss!

✈   ✈   ✈   ✈   ✈

12 Million Golf Balls!—A substantial advertising campaign accompanied introduction of the Boeing 707. Taking advantage of its popular appeal and the fact that it was America's first jet passenger transport to go into service, a number of tie-ins with other advertisers were arranged.

We tied in only with well-known companies and quality products, even insisting on extensive tests of some products. Hathaway brought out a "Lady Hathaway 707 shirt," each shirt carrying a tag extolling the Boeing 707. We tied in with Zenith radio only after actually demonstrating that it had fine reception while flying at 25,000 feet in a 707.

An internationally-known watch company wanted to tie in with its expensive, multi-purpose wristwatch. We agreed, provided that our test pilots would approve the watch for test flight use. A dozen of the watches were sent to us and distributed among the flight crews. The crews unanimously agreed that the watches were excellent for their needs.

On day I received a call from the Wilson golf ball people. They proposed naming their new golf ball the

707 Jet Flight. We were asked if we had an artist who could help design the display boxes which would hold the balls at the dealers' points of sale.

Keith Kinsman, public relations art director, was assigned the design task. He came up with a three-ball carton and another holding a dozen balls.

Boeing 707 was applied in every possible combination. You just couldn't set the cartons up without the Boeing name appearing.

A bit curious as to procedure, I asked the Wilson representative what kind of numbers were involved. He replied: "Our first run will be a million dozen."

Shortly before he retired from all activity with the company, I gave the last carton of three balls to Bill Allen. I explained that the balls were nearly 20 years old and doubtless could not be driven more than 25 yards. "That's just about my distance these days," Bill replied.

✈ ✈ ✈ ✈ ✈

Love Those Nurses—Barely two years after joining Boeing in 1942, I suffered an involuntary six-weeks' sojourn in Swedish Hospital. My purpose is not to relate details of my operation but to sing paens of praise for that oft-maligned individual, the hospital nurse. Cheerful under the most adverse conditions, tolerant of the idiosyncrasies of the ill, understanding of fear, yet stern when the situation requires, and feisty at times—that's my nurse!

Jackie was my favorite. Laser beams danced from her black eyes. Peaches and cream complexion. A sexy laugh that developed deep behind her tonsils. She was forthright in expressing feelings and reactions, yet had an ability to catch the humor of a given situation. And certainly nature had not shorted her when it came to distribution of feminine accoutrement.

The president of one of Seattle's largest banks had been admitted to the hospital with a mild heart attack and was placed in the room next to mine. From the constant comings and goings, it was obvious that he was demanding an inordinate amount of attention.

Two days later Jackie came into my room, the laser beams strong enough to burn holes in a steel plate, heels clicking a flamenco. I didn't have to ask. Jackie exclaimed: "That old son of a bitch next door. He's an ass-pincher!" and she stormed into my bathroom for a calming cigarette.

Another day and Jackie was more herself—giggly. She could hardly contain her mirth as she entered my room.

"Okay, Jackie, what is it this time?" I said.

"I've been helping out the 'aides' this morning with baths. I was doing that milquetoast down in 511. Right by the book. Chest. Back. Right arm. Left arm. Right leg. Left leg. Then I soaped up the washcloth real good, handed it to him and told him to finish his bath. I stepped out so he wouldn't be embarrassed as he followed, I presumed, normal procedure. After a few minutes I went back in and he had shampooed his hair!" And Jackie went off into another burst of laughter.

One day one of the regular nurses declared: "Have we got something special for you tomorrow. Wait until you see the gorgeous redhead assigned to give you your bath."

With a shortage of nurses, many of whom had gone off to join the military or to work at Boeing, civilian "nurses' aides" volunteers had been enlisted to assist the harried RNs. At Swedish most morning bath duties were assigned these aides. All day the build-up continued about my upcoming bath.

The next morning a couple of nurses seemed to have continuing business in my room about bath time. "You're next," one declared.

My door opened. And there was a ravishing redhead, doing full justice to the build-up. Stacked! Gorgeous gluteus maximus! Most dated girl on the UW campus a few years earlier. I was shocked.

"Good lord, Peggy," I exclaimed. "When we were at the U who would have thought that some day you would be giving me a bath."

"That isn't all," she replied. "I have you down for an enema!"

✦ ✦ ✦ ✦ ✦

Tough Job—One of the many pleasures in public relations operations was the selection of models for various publicity and advertising photography. We selected many models from within Boeing's plentiful ranks of good-looking young ladies. For night shots and for extended photographic sessions we used professional models.

Kathleen Peck, who maintained a local modeling school, provided many models for us. So it was rather normal when Kathleen called me one day to report that she was staging a fashion show at Frederick and Nelson. She suggested that I come up to the luncheon affair, as she had some new models I might like to look over against future needs. I've said this was a tough job.

In the center of Frederick's tearoom, where the fashion shows were held, was a large round table, seating 20 or so. It was reserved for men only. Apparently more men than one would think are hooked on fashion shows. I took a place at the table shortly before the parade of models began. Among the girls were a number whom we had used previously. Seeing me at the table, several came by, smiled sweetly and greeted me personally. This went on for some time when a man across from me threw down his napkin and said emphatically, "Damn it, what have you got that I haven't got?"

✈ ✈ ✈ ✈ ✈

Scotch Luggage—Product and employment advertising were a substantial operation of Boeing's public relations department. National advertising was handled by N.W. Ayer and Son, well-known Philadelphia agency. Employment advertising and local Seattle advertising was handled by Frederick E. Baker and Associates. Bill Coldren was on the public relations staff as advertising manager.

Baker and Coldren were in San Francisco as the first step to a meeting in New York with the Ayer people and Harold Mansfield, in conjunction with his book *Vision*.

In order to be prepared adequately for cold weather in New York, or possible snakebite, Coldren had procured a bottle of scotch, only to discover that he did not have room for it in his luggage. Baker volunteered to put it in his bag.

When they recovered their luggage after off-planing in New York, Baker was handed a bag which reeked of scotch. Obviously the bottle had been broken in transit handling. The taxi driver and the bellhop at the hotel both cast suspicious and questioning glances at Baker and his luggage.

In his room Baker discovered that the liquor had

seeped throughout his bag, lending an aura of heather and the highlands to the contents. Further, his bag itself retained a high aroma of scotch. Clothing was sent out for a thorough cleaning. The bag, however, continued to perfume the entire room.

It had been arranged that the next morning Mansfield, already registered at the hotel, would come to Baker's room for breakfast and conference.

Baker phoned Mansfield: "Harold, could we meet in your room instead of mine. The maid doesn't seem to be available and my room is a mess."

Mansfield agreed on the transfer. I believe that this is the first he will learn of the reason for the shift in meeting place. It took some good clean Puget Sound air to finally rid Baker's bag of its redolence.

13

Flight Test

Slim and Tex—two who shook up management

One for Guinness—As the Boeing XC-97 was about to take off from Seattle on January 9, 1945, on what was hoped would be a new transcontinental speed record, I made a $5 bet with Al Miller of the sales staff.

The XC-97 was the prototype for a military transport. Elliott Merrill and John Fornesero were at the controls as the big plane headed east on the most direct route to Washington, DC. Sixteen Boeing and military personnel were aboard.

By the time we neared Missoula, Montana, in a little over 90 minutes, we had climbed to 30,000 feet, made possible by supercharging of the engines and pressurization of the entire fuselage. The interior altitude was a comfortable 8,000 feet.

From up in the cockpit with its bird's-eye view, Missoula lay directly ahead. Behind the town on a mountainside, the big "M" of the University of Montana could be seen. Off to the left was Helena, state capital, and ahead and a little to the right, Butte and Deer Lodge. The latter my old home town.

On we sped in the smooth air of the upper atmosphere. Over South Dakota, just south of Chicago, then over Illinois and Indiana. Let-down for the landing at Washington was started over Columbus, Ohio, some 300 miles out. With permission, Elliott buzzed the Washington National Airport tower to record our exact time—6 hours, 3 minutes and 30 seconds! A new transcontinental speed record!

"Okay, Al, pay me," I said. I had won our bet. I had become the first person to cross the United States without visiting the restroom!

✈ ✈ ✈ ✈ ✈

Down-the-Up-Stairs—Following the transcontinental speed dash, the XC-97 was put on display at Washington airport. The plane had clamshell doors at the rear through which ramps could be let down. Trucks and similar equipment could be driven up the ramps and direct into the aircraft.

The unobstructed cabin was as long as a bowling alley. At the forward end, just aft of the cockpit, a vertical ladder led down to the lower cargo hold and a short four-step ramp to the ground.

The viewing public was being directed up the ramp at the rear, through the airplane, with a look into the cockpit and then down the forward ladder and out.

As I was directing the steady flow of visitors, I

noticed a good-looking young lady attempting to leave by the rear ramp up which she had entered the plane. Down-the-up-stairs as it were.

"Sorry, you can't leave that way. You will have to go forward and down the ladder like all the other people."

"I've got to go back down the ramp," she declared.

"Sorry, no can do."

"Look," she said, "I've got to go down that way. I can't go down the ladder. I don't have any pants on!"

I stopped the traffic and escorted her down the ramp. Since the January temperature was below freezing, I just couldn't understand her coming out, well, sort of bare-headed.

✈ ✈ ✈ ✈ ✈

Tex and the Bust Warfare—Boeing's part in the great TV bust warfare was unplanned and squelched before it got under way. Older readers will recall the TV star, she of the most generous upstairs endowment, or is it endowments. She was an English girl, and American film makers could not permit this challenge to American pulchritude. With judicious use of tape measures, an American champion was selected—a movie starlet whose name I forget. A tremendous publicity program was devoted to her.

Quite unrelated to any of these shenanigans, Boeing sales had arranged a demonstration flight of the Dash-80 to Los Angeles. I went along to represent public relations and was sitting in the jump seat behind Tex Johnston, the pilot, when we taxied into a designated parking place beside the main passenger terminal.

As Tex and Dix Loesch, co-pilot, were tidying the cockpit, I glanced out the window. Rolling toward us was a topless Ford Thunderbird, completely covered with leopard skin. As the car squealed to a halt, a gorgeous blonde leaped out and started running toward the plane, jiggling provocatively at every step, truly a titular contender—Miss America bust! The driver of the car, laden with cameras, was at her heels.

The girl was shouting something to me. Looking down, I observed, "Tex, have you ever flown over the Grand Canyon and looked down into its depths? If not, come over here."

When the loading stairs had been wheeled into place at the front door, the girl and the photog dashed up. They wanted to take a picture of the gal sitting on Tex's lap in the cockpit yet! I said, "Absolutely no way. Por nada. Nyet, Nien." Strange action for a public relations person.

I think Tex was disappointed.

✈ ✈ ✈ ✈ ✈

The "100" Comes Home—Old Boeing planes don't die, nor like General MacArthur do they just fade away; they become classics. Typical of the genre is the first Model 100, which after a highly varied history has come back home to Boeing Field. In production, Model 100 became the famed P-12 fighter.

Boeing sold the first Model 100 to Pratt and Whitney to be used as a test bed for the engine which would power the P-12s. After the tests were completed, P and W sold the plane to Milo Birchman, who barnstormed his flying circus all over the country. Flying the 100, he won the world aerobatic competition in 1936. Later he sold the plane to Joe Thorne, who stored it in a Los Angeles hangar, where it was damaged when a roof caved in. Paul Mantz, noted movie stunt flyer, added the plane to his collection used in making movies.

When Mantz was killed during filming of "Flight of the Phoenix," his planes were auctioned and the 100 was acquired by a man in Florida. He in turn sold it to an airline pilot who attempted to restore it.

Lou Wallick, then director of Boeing Flight Test operations, learned of the 100's availability, and in partnership with Bob Muckelstone, Seattle attorney, bought the plane and had it trucked to Seattle. They found that much more than 50 percent restoration was necessary. The work was done by Orville Tosh, former Alaska bush pilot, who had a shop on Boeing Field.

It was a champagne-toast day when Wallick took up the restored plane for its first test flight. The powerful little plane leaped into the air after a run of only 300 or 400 feet. Wallick circled the field twice and at the request of the control tower personnel, flew low past them so they could have a close-up of the plane.

Later Wallick flew the 100 cross-country to Oshkosh, Wisconsin, for that city's famed annual fly-in. Some 10,000 planes take part in the fly-in each year. The 100 was one of the featured attractions as old-timers identified the fantastic little plane as the P-12. Later Wallick flew the plane to classic aircraft shows in Watsonville and Merced, California, as well as to Evergreen in Oregon and Abbotsford in British Columbia.

The 100 is now on display at the Museum of Flight located on Boeing Field, Seattle, where it has joined the B and W, 247, 80A, B-47 and other Boeing planes which didn't fade away.

✈ ✈ ✈ ✈ ✈

Smart Thinking—It was a red-letter day for Bob Lamson, Boeing engineer and test pilot. First, he had just become the father of a baby daughter, Wendy. Second, he was to run high-speed taxi tests on the XF8B, a radical new Navy fighter with super-powerful engine and counter-rotating propellers.

The schedule for the day called for a series of tests, checking controls and braking. A final run to be made at maximum speed, just under take-off speed.

"On this final run I gradually brought the plane up to max ground speed," Lamson relates. "In fact, I had to raise the tail to keep from taking off. Just as I reached top speed, the plane slewed violently to the right. My first thought was that someone was running up a plane's engine in one of the revetments lining the runway and the propeller blast had hit me.

"I gave full left rudder, squared the wings and was actually off the ground a few inches. As the plane settled back, there was a horrible clank and bang as the propellers hit the concrete runway. Somehow the landing gear had come up. We slid to a stop on bent props and the partially retracted landing gear.

"Ground crew and engineers who had been checking the run dashed up. 'What happened?' they asked. I had to admit that I didn't know. One of the engineers climbed up and looked into the cockpit. 'Well, Bob's in the clear. The gear handle is still down and locked.' 'Not necessarily so,' Earl Jensen observed. 'Could have been smart thinking.'"

Bob explains that the Navy specified hydraulic

systems for landing gear, while the Boeing systems were electrical and automatically retracted when the weight came off the gear. When the plane lifted a few inches off the runway, the gear automatically retracted.

June Lamson adds her bit to the day's history. "I was still half groggy after Wendy's birth when a nurse rushed in. 'Are you the Mrs. Lamson whose husband just crashed on Boeing Field?' she asked."

Level heads made a quick check with Boeing and assured June that Bob was okay. The unthinking nurse was wisely transferred to duties where she had no direct patient contact.

✈ ✈ ✈ ✈ ✈

Bail Out—Taking to their parachutes was a unique experience for a Boeing experimental flight test crew headed by Elliott Merrill, pilot, with Ken Luplow as a crew member. Theirs was one of only three planes lost from hundreds of experimental and production planes Boeing flight tested during World War II. The specific B-17 test had been ordered by the Air Force.

The test was initiated high over the Olympic peninsula. In a high-speed dive, part of the test, fabric fasteners on the empennage came off, causing the tail to fail. The plane went into an uncontrollable spin. Merrill ordered the crew to bail out. He left last. As he drifted down in his parachute, the spinning plane whirled perilously close to him. Plane and pilot landed less than 100 yards apart in a farmer's field.

Others of the crew were scattered widely over the peninsula. Luplow had a habit of loosely tying his shoe laces. When his 'chute opened, he was snapped out of his shoes. He drifted down to land in the top of a high fir tree. He hung there for some time when, fortunately, a timber cruiser came through the area and spotted the hung-up flier.

"Can you get me something to cut these shroud lines?" Luplow asked. "Only way I can get down." The cruiser climbed an adjacent tree and tossed a large pocket knife over to Luplow. Clean miss! The knife clattered to the ground, where the timberman reclaimed it. Second try was successful. Luplow caught the knife, cut himself free and slid down the fir.

Meantime, company officials, alerted by radio of the impending crash, cruised the area, picking up one crew member here, another there, two at a crossroads grocery store and finally Luplow. He had walked out through the woods for a half mile, trodding gingerly on roots and forest debris in his stocking feet.

No one was hurt. The plane burned on impact. Luplow from that time onward was very careful to tie his shoelaces with double knots.

✈ ✈ ✈ ✈ ✈

Slim Too—Tex Johnston was not the first Boeing test pilot to cause consternation among company executives through unprogrammed maneuvers with a new type aircraft.

The Model 200—the Monomail—was first flown by test pilot Eddie Allen. Later Slim Lewis came up from Wyoming to do additional testing. Monty Monteith, chief engineer, and others went to the plant rooftop to watch.

After Lewis had made a number of steep banks, they saw him go into a dive, pour on the power and then pull up sharply. Monteith clasped his hands over his head, "Oh, no, he wouldn't dare! The plane won't stand it!" Up, up and over on his back went Lewis in a perfect loop. Not only once, he repeated the maneuver two more times!

Maybe Tex was only carrying on a tradition established by Slim Lewis long before the Dash-80 roll.

✈ ✈ ✈ ✈ ✈

Tex Reacts—Early flight tests of the Dash-80—the 707 prototype—had gone well, and Tex Johnston and his crew were very pleased, as were the various engineers and management people on the project.

As part of final testing, Tex made repeated high-speed taxi runs to near take-off speed, then braked severely. Knowing that the brakes were superhot, Tex took off to cool them by flying about a bit. After a half-hour Tex radioed that he was returning to the field.

Approaching Boeing Field from the south for a north landing on Runway 31, Tex touched down right on the numbers (as he usually did) and stepped on the brakes. Nothing happened!

"I immediately checked to see if I had nose steering. If not, I was going to go around, pull up the main gear and come in for a belly landing," Tex states.

Fifteen million dollars' worth of test airplane, the only one of its kind, in imminent danger of serious damage or complete loss!

"I decided to try a big looping turn and come back down the runway," Tex adds. "There wasn't too much room. Boeing planes lined the west side of the field, with private planes and the old terminal on the east side."

The plane rolled ahead, slowing slightly. Opposite the old passenger terminal, at the field's widest point, Tex started a big circle, still at some 80 miles an hour. The maneuver was going well until a large mound of concrete, discarded from a paving job and hidden in the weeds, interposed itself. The nose wheel of the plane hit the mound squarely and was sheared off. The Dash-80 slid ahead on its nose in an unusual and unbeautiful position.

Emergency equipment dashed across the field. Supervisors rushed up in cars and trucks. Others came running afoot. As the crowd pushed closer to the stricken craft, the left-hand cockpit window slowly slid back and Tex stuck his head out surveying the damage. He summed up his exasperation and frustration in just two words, "Oh, shit!"

✦ ✦ ✦ ✦ ✦

Tex Rolls the Dash-80—In the mid-1950s hydroplane racing fever was at a peak in Seattle. In July 1954 some 300,000 fans had gathered on the shores of Lake Washington to witness the Gold Cup races.

A meeting of IATA and AIA, two major aviation industry groups, were scheduled in Seattle during race week. Most of the aviation people stayed over after their sessions to watch the speedboats perform. Boeing chartered three yachts from which the visitors could witness the spectacle.

I was assigned to the yacht on which Bill Allen was the Boeing host. Among guests were Dutch Kindleberger, president of North American Aviation, T. Claude Ryan of Ryan Aircraft and Rocky Rochlin from Douglas public relations.

Boeing had just developed and was test flying the Dash-80, swept-wing prototype for America's first jet transport, the 707. Bill Allen had asked Tex Johnston to fly the Dash-80 over the race course between race heats so that the assembled multitude could see this radical new aircraft and, I suspect, to alert the competition to what lay ahead.

Tex had been doing test work out over the Olympic peninsula, so at the agreed time he came across the lake headed southwest, did a chandelle followed by a roll, leveled off and flew the length of the race course before pulling up in another roll. One could sense gasps from the shore-side assemblage.

"Say, Rocky," I said to my friend Rocklin from Douglas, "have you folks rolled the DC-8?" "Wise guy," Rocky answered, for Douglas had not yet flown its challenger to Boeing's jet.

I had just turned away when Mr. Allen motioned to me. "I don't think we should have anything about that in the newspapers," he said.

"Gee, Bill, look over there," and I pointed to the shore. "Three hundred thousand people just saw that roll. No one could keep it out of the papers."

Pete Jansen, production genius, who had been with Bill Knudsen on the War Production Board, and now a Boeing consultant, broke in with his Danish accent, "Don't worry, Bill, he's done that before."

Boeing engineers in the plane said that Tex held it in a perfect one "G" roll. Tex explains that a plane doesn't know if it is flying level or on its back. It only responds to "G" forces. At one "G" in the roll, the stresses were no greater than in level flight.

Surprisingly nothing of the maneuver appeared in either of the local papers the next day. It certainly wasn't because of any public relations plea, as we knew it would have been futile to try to kill such a story. I guess the omission was a reflection of Seattle's mania with hydroplanes in that day, compared to interest even in radical new airplanes.

Later, as Boeing dominated the jet transport market, many airline executives said they had been highly impressed with the design and construction integrity of a commercial airplane which could be rolled with confidence. Those rolls sold, and are still selling, a lot of airplanes. No other commercial transport has been so demonstrated.

Allen, of course, had concern for the $15 million of company funds invested in the jet project. He told Tex what he thought of the caper in mighty positive terms. And he remained adamant in his position.

A year later T Wilson and Tex were chatting at Allen's annual management lawn party when Allen walked up. Smiling, Tex said, "Bill, will you admit now that that Dash-80 roll was good for sales?" According to T, "Bill got that cold steel look in his eyes, said an emphatic 'No,' turned on his heel and walked away."

✈ ✈ ✈ ✈ ✈

Navigation Simplified—The 707 was scheduled for a demonstration flight to Venezuela. Tex Johnston, as usual, was the pilot. As the plane hadn't been flown to that South American country before, I was curious about the navigation problem.

"Tex, how are you going to navigate down to Caracas when you haven't been there before?"

"Easy," he replied. "You just fly east until you hit the Atlantic Ocean, then you turn right."

Ask a silly question . . .

✈ ✈ ✈ ✈ ✈

Private Air Show—"Bomb tossing" was one of the techniques perfected during World War II. A B-47 would go into a dive from considerable altitude and just as it pulled out, it would release its bomb which would follow a parabolic flight to the target. In the meantime, the B-47 would climb sharply to avoid results of the bomb's explosion at the target.

Tests of the toss technique were carried out by Wichita test pilots who dropped the bombs on a remote Kansas area. The tests went on for a number of successive days, until it was decided to skip a day.

A long distance call came from an irate farmer. Seems he had invited friends for the customary "air show," that no planes had shown up and he wanted to know when the next "air show" was scheduled.

✈   ✈   ✈   ✈   ✈

Tex and his Lion—Tex Johnston had gone to San Diego to be fitted for a crash helmet. They couldn't be bought off the shelf in those days. At the same time Boeing had won a contract for the KC-97. To celebrate the event, Tex was at the Koana Kai club where he met Phil Coffer, president of MetalCal, and others of his friends.

The second evening of his stay in San Diego, Tex returned to his cabana at a resort on the waterfront. He opened his door to find a cage containing a half-grown lion in the center of the room.

"She looked friendly, so I let her out of the cage and gave her some water in an ashtray," Tex says. "She settled down in a corner and I went to bed."

The next morning Tex joined the friends of the night before for an eye-opener at the bar. They all gave indications of a suppressed excitement.

"Anything unusual last night, Tex, when you went to your room?" one asked. Another inquired, "Sleep all right?"

"No, nothing unusual I can think of," Tex replied casually. "Oh, there was a lion in my room. I made her sleep in a corner. I slept like a log."

A few days later Coffer had the lion re-crated and flown to Seattle. There she was delivered to Tex's home on Hunt's Point. The crate was placed in the family play-room. When the crate was opened, the lion, which Tex had named "Mach II," wouldn't come out. So Delores, Tex's wife, took the animal by the collar and coaxed her out.

When grown to considerably larger size, Mach II was given to the Seattle zoo. There she presented the zoo with five litters of cubs over the years.

14

New York-
Washington

The "Tuesday Musical"—unique Public Relations group

Mountsier's Threat—In the first stages of its expanding commercial airplane business, Boeing used the national public relations services of its advertising agency. Later it established its own New York office with Miss Florence Teets in charge. Among the various aviation editors with whom Florence dealt was Robert Mountsier, of the now defunct *New York Sun*. Mountsier was a dignified gentleman in both action and appearance. He insisted his name be pronounced "Mont-seer," not "Montsewer."

One day at a large gathering of aviation people at

the Wings Club, Florence made the mistake of intro-
ducing the *Sun* editor as "Mr. Mountsewer." Later he
came over to her table and said in his dignified
manner, "Miss Teets, the next time you mispronounce
my name I shall mispronounce yours." Touché!

✈ ✈ ✈ ✈ ✈

Overdrive Mark—After a hiatus of a year following Miss Teets' departure, the New York office was
reestablished with Mark Nevils in charge. Mark was
hard-working, hyper-energetic and traveled in overdrive high at all times. Keeping up with him as he
made the rounds in New York would have been good
training for the Boston marathon. In addition to his
New York duties, Mark spent an average two days a
week in the Washington office. His recall of amusing
and unusual occurrences is phenomenal.

As one of the features of its sales promotion
program, Boeing had a full-scale mock-up of the 707
interior constructed in a warehouse on the New York
waterfront. The main cabin was fully furnished with
reclining seats, restroom facilities and even a public
address system.

Nevils was frequently called on to brief the advertising agencies and staff personnel of customer airlines on the features of the mock-up. On one occasion
he was talking to some 20 representatives of the
airline of one of the emerging nations. He was surprised and nonplussed at the number of questions he
received regarding the 707's toilet facilities.

When the lecture was over, the head of the airline's advertising agency explained to Nevils: "Don't
be surprised at all those questions you were asked

about the toilets. In their native land they are still using corn cobs."

✈ ✈ ✈ ✈ ✈

When the president of Royal Air Morocco and his wife were to arrive in New York on their way to Seattle, Nevils was asked to meet them. Sales explained that although both were fluent in French, neither spoke much English. However, they wished to see a Broadway play, hear some jazz music, visit Harlem and do some shopping.

"I obtained scalper's tickets to 'Hair,'" Nevils reports, "took them to hear Jimmy Ryan's jazz and had difficulty persuading a taxi driver to take us to Harlem. How to handle the shopping tour was a problem as I didn't speak French. Fortunately, my daughter Kathy was knowledgeable in 'academic French' and later received her Master's degree in marketing at a French university in Versailles, France. The president and his wife were so pleased with Kathy's assistance that they extended her a standing invitation to visit Casablanca and they personally would take her through the Casbah."

Kathy should have been on the Boeing payroll. She performed still another interpreter-guide service when the president of Air Madagascar and his wife, enroute to Seattle, stopped over in New York to do some shopping.

"I explained the situation to Kathy," Nevils relates, "gave her some money to take the wife to luncheon and introduced the pair. That evening Kathy reported that they had toured Lord and Taylor, Saks Fifth Avenue, Altman and other exclusive shops.

They were crossing 42nd Street when they passed one of those restaurants which feature a chef in the window tossing flapjacks. Enthralled, that's where Kathy's guest wanted to eat, and they did!"

✈ ✈ ✈ ✈ ✈

Before joining Boeing, Nevils had handled public relations for both Curtis-Wright and Eastern Airlines. When with C-W he was assigned to cover flight tests of the twin-engine C-W 20, which later became the popular Commando.

Famed test pilot Eddie Allen had been hired by C–W to do the testing of the new plane. As the initial flight date approached, Nevils learned that feisty Ted Wagner, aviation editor of the St. Louis *Post-Dispatch* had arranged a private interview with Allen.

Fearing that such an interview would get Curtis-Wright in dutch with the competing St. Louis *Globe-Democrat*, Nevils expressed his doubts about such a session. Allen assured Nevils that he would say nothing to embarrass C-W. Wagner held his interview and left. When no story appeared and weeks passed, Nevils asked Wagner about it. Wagner replied: "Allen was most friendly and cooperative. He answered all my questions. But his answers were so damn technical I couldn't decide what he was talking about. So, no story!"

✈ ✈ ✈ ✈ ✈

Jim Beats a General—Like most large companies having substantial business with the government, Boeing maintains a Washington, DC, office. For years it was in charge of Jim Murray, naval aviator in World War I and early day airmail pilot. In his airmail days Jim flew what was known as the toughest leg of the San Francisco-Chicago route, the leg from Salt Lake City to Cheyenne, Wyoming. On one occasion forced down on the high prairie by a blizzard, Jim taxied his plane 30 miles to his Cheyenne terminal.

Soft spoken, just under average height, Jim was the epitome of a perfect gentleman. He was a member of the very exclusive Burning Tree Country Club, favorite golf course of senators, top Pentagon brass and Washington business leaders. Somewhere along the line he had taken up golf and with his usual thoroughness had mastered the game to the point where he played to a two handicap. He was a favored playing opponent of generals and admirals. At least one loser of a hefty wager is said to have remarked, "I don't mind losing, but I hate to get beat by such a little fart!"

Jim and Mark Nevils, in Washington on his weekly visit, had driven to the airport to meet Bill Allen. On the way to town Nevils facetiously remarked, "Mr. Allen, I don't think Mr. Murray is doing much for Boeing public relations. He has just beaten and eliminated General Twining (at that time head of the Air Force) in the club tournament at Burning Tree.

Jim seriously explained, "Bill, I just couldn't help it. I tried not to make Nate look bad, but if I had pulled any shots, he certainly would have noted and resented it."

✈ ✈ ✈ ✈ ✈

Beall the Host—Wellwood Beall was the consummate host when entertaining at his home or afield. On this particular occasion in Washington, DC, he was entertaining four or five generals and admirals and their wives. He had also asked Mark Nevils, who happened to be in Washington, and Jim Murray, head of Boeing's Washington office, to join the party.

Beall selected a highly unusual restaurant of the old-fashioned "saloon" type. It was heavy with atmosphere—nude sketches on the walls, a brass rail at the bar under which there was a trough with running water and, visible upstairs, the doors to a number of rooms.

At intervals during the dinner Beall gave his guests, in groups of two or three, a guided tour of the place. He explained what the trough was for, how the upstairs rooms were used for masculine "relaxation" and how in the earlier days General Ulysses S. Grant was a regular customer and how President Lincoln used to page Grant there. The guests, particularly the women, were greatly entertained by Beall's lecture tour.

Some time later Nevils, again in Washington, encountered his old friend Jack McCoy, the famed aircraft artist. Jack liked to eat and also had a preference for "atmosphere."

"So I decided to take him to the restaurant where Beall had intrigued his guests," Nevils recalls. "I repeated to Jack all that Beall had told us, possibly embellishing a bit. I even mentioned the Lincoln and Grant episodes.

"Jack was more interested in the nude sketches and wondered what the artist had received for executing them. I summoned the maitre d' and told him of Jack's interest. He said he wasn't sure but likely the artist just received food and drink for his work. Then, leaning over the table, he said to me, 'Look, my friend, I had better explain to you that this place wasn't even built when Lincoln and Grant were around.'

"That's when I concluded that Beall was a helluva salesman."

✈ ✈ ✈ ✈ ✈

Tuesday Musical—The Tuesday Musical is a unique organization of military, public relations and press personnel. From its headquarters in Washington, DC, it has chapters throughout the world. Hawaii has its ukelele and lei chapter, Tokyo its sake and semisan, while Seattle has its oboe and zither chapter. Boeing has been represented in both the Seattle and Washington, DC, chapters.

The club charter provides: "No singing, no officers, no rules, no Tuesday meetings, no objections and absolutely no plans." The organization has one major achievement to its credit. It is directly responsible for Smokey the Bear. A number of years ago the press featured a story about an orphan cub bear whose mother had been killed in a Rocky Mountain forest fire. Club members proposed that the cub be brought to Washington and presented to the National Zoo. Since one of the members was the top public relations officer of the Air Force, there was no problem in arranging for an Air Force plane to bring the cub to Washington. He was aptly named "Smokey" and became the model for the Forest Service's campaign to prevent forest fires.

The Washington chapter invested in one share of stock in each of a number of aerospace companies in order to "have a voice in management." Dick Boutelle, president of the Fairchild Company, begged the group to cash its three or four cent dividend checks in order to clear the company books. Boutelle later scored a counter victory.

He invited the Washington group to Hagerstown for an evening bash. He cautioned it was "men only" and he would provide feminine companions for the evening.

"Have to work late at the office," "Visitor has to be met," "Boss calling an evening meeting," were among the explanations given wives to account for the evening absence.

At the banquet room, after a couple of drinks had been served, Boutelle explained that the feminine company for the evening was hidden on the stage. The curtain would be raised, only to the feminine knees, and the members were to make their selection from that viewpoint.

"Me for dimple-knees on the right," "I like fourth from the left," "I go for the light brown nylons" were some of the selections. When all choices had been made, the curtain was slowly, very slowly raised—to reveal the wives of the assembled Tuesday Musical members.

Boutelle had gathered the wives, sworn them to secrecy and brought them to Hagerstown.

"Ah, we knew it was a gag all the time," proved a not very effective explanation. More lawns were mowed, windows washed and household chores accomplished that weekend than had been the norm for several months.

A major event of the Washington chapter each year is a boat trip and beer party down the Potomac on May 1. Its purpose is to "celebrate the day that sex moved outdoors."

✦ ✦ ✦ ✦ ✦

Wrong Chart—Murray and his assistant, Cliff Roberts, were in Seattle for a conference and the annual physical examination required of all management personnel. Roberts disappeared and returned to Washington. Murray later learned that Roberts was told his examination revealed a serious medical condition and that he should return at once to Washington for treatment.

Cliff had barely reached Washington when a Boeing medic phoned him to explain that there had been a mix-up in X-ray charts, and he actually was in perfect condition.

I could sympathize with Cliff. In one of my post-exam interview the doctor said, "Now we don't want you to be alarmed, but the chart here shows a peculiarity in your heart beat. Here it is right—say, this isn't your chart!"

"Gee, thanks a million, doc. If I didn't have an off-beat before I'm sure I have one now!"

15

Public
Relations
Types

Zany romantics, somehow they got the job done

Those Zany P.R. Types—The staff of the *Boeing News*, employee weekly newspaper headed by By Fish and the art department, under Keith Kinsman, had been shunted to the boondocks of the leased Kenworth plant because of war-time shortage of space. The two groups were uninhibited and free-wheeling. Unorthodox best describes their operations.

With great care and unusual realism, Kinsman and his artists molded a 2-foot long snake from modeling clay. It was painted bright colors and proper beady eyes were applied. The snake was carefully coiled in the "In" mail basket, and a fine, invisible thread was run from the basket, across the low ceiling, to Fish's desk. When the mail girl came in to deliver her load, Fish pulled the string and the snake reared up. The girl dropped her mail and jumped back, mumbling, "Uh, uh, uh," then fled. She refused to deliver any more mail to that office.

✈ ✈ ✈ ✈ ✈

Just a Small Nail—After the war Fish went back to free-lancing and his column in the *Seattle Times*. Kinsman and his art group, along with the remaining newspaper staff, were moved back to the DPC annex in the headquarters area, where a bit more supervision was possible.

I laid down the law. "Now look, you clowns, you are back in civilization. No more horseplay. No more nude pictures on the walls. No nails to hang pictures on. No tricks on mail girls."

Duly noted, and decorum reigned for almost a week. Out of slight curiosity and some reasonable business at hand, I went across the street to the new quarters. After visiting the photo lab, I walked toward Kinsman's office. To my horror I saw the sharp end of a large spike protruding through the wall, its pointed end sticking out 3 or 4 inches. I stepped into the office, and there on the other side of the wall was the head of the spike, at least 6 inches in length.

"What goes on here?" I demanded. "Who did this? I'll get plant protection to run this down!"

"Well, gee, we just wanted to hang a bit of our art work," Kinsman said. "That little nail bother you? I'll fix it." He went over and lifted the offending spike from the wall.

Those characters had fashioned a spike out of cardboard, cut it in two and glued the respective segments in perfect alignment outside and inside the wall. With gleeful anticipation they had awaited my visit to their new quarters. Got the old man!

✈ ✈ ✈ ✈ ✈

A Taste for Oreos—During the 10-hour work shifts in practice during World War II, it was customary for employees to take 15-minute coffee breaks, morning and afternoon. The routine was followed by the *Boeing News* and art staffs of public relations. The crews would gather in one of the offices and, over coffee, share purchased or homemade goodies. A particular favorite was Oreos, those crisp chocolate cookies with a creamy white filling.

One of the chaps had the habit of concentrating on the Oreos, devouring most of them before others had a chance at the delicacy. Keith Kinsman, the art director, decided the situation needed correction. He procured a supply of the Oreos, separated a number into two parts, scraped off the sugared white filling. He then replaced the filling with white library paste, such as is used in kindergartens and other juvenile enterprises.

The next day the paste-filled cookies were put out at the coffee break. The Oreo fiend, with apparent relish, ate the full complement. Kinsman got out additional cookies and his paste pot. He spread another cookie and handed it over. Only then did the culprit realize what he had been eating. At all future coffee breaks he eschewed participation in the Oreos.

✈ ✈ ✈ ✈ ✈

Flat on His Back—How he got into our collection of unreconstructed public relations zanies is not clear; nevertheless here was this chap, 100 percent serious, disdainful of the rompings of the characters around him. At lunch time he ate a sandwich at his desk, then went to work on a self project, perfectly legitimate since he was on his own time.

Our offices were lit by a series of overhead lights from which hung off and on chains. These chains came down to about a foot above an average man's head. It was an ongoing game to see if anyone could kick high enough to touch one of the chains.

Such a contest went on several days in succession just outside the office of Mr. Serious. He pretended no interest, but it was noted that he took an occasional sly peek. On one or two occasions, those returning from lunch noted a suspicious movement of one of the chains. It was suspected that perhaps Mr. Serious was more interested in the kick game than he indicated.

The next day the group made an ostentatious display of departing for lunch, but instead concealed themselves in an adjoining office, leaving the door slightly ajar. Before doing so, they surreptitiously shortened the light chain by a good six inches.

Sure enough! With a careful look around, Mr. Serious came out and attempted a kick. Missed. Tried it again, and, good lord, he made it, starting the chain swaying. But with one leg high in the air, the other went out from under him and he crashed on his back. Knocked out cold!

The sobered and contrite witnesses rushed out and with words of encouragement and application of cold compresses brought the victim around. He insisted, and continued to maintain religiously, that he had slipped on a wet spot on the floor. "Damn poor maintenance around here, leaving slippery spots like that," he groused for several days.

✈ ✈ ✈ ✈ ✈

Steuben for a Collector—What could one do with that spike-through-the-wall, Oreo cookie, free-wheeling public relations gang? They did an excellent job in their respective areas, so it was hard to censure them and more difficult to lessen their shenanigans.

Their machinations pursued me even in my retirement. My "You're out-of-a-job" party was held in the Spanish Ballroom of the Olympic Hotel. I was honored and amazed at the turnout. On the other hand, perhaps there was general joy that I was leaving.

I had insisted that there be no gold watch business and no speeches. When I discovered that Keith Kinsman and Vern Rutledge were to preside as masters of ceremonies, I prepared for the worst. A 2-foot high loving cup, engraved to "The Iron Duke" (their favorite title for me because of certain hard-headed budget dictates) was presented. The cup had originally been awarded to the winner of airplane speed races in Baltimore. My friends had found it in a second-hand store on First Avenue. How it got to Seattle was a mystery. Other gags followed the award.

Finally Vern said, "This has been fun. But, now enough of this foolishness. There is one person who has had to live with the man we honor question mark for many years. So, in a serious moment we want to give proper recognition to his wife Harriet. We have discovered that she is very fond of, and a collector of, Steuben glass. Certainly nothing could be more suitable for one with such discerning taste. If Harriet will come up here to the platform, Kinsman has a special presentation for her from the entire staff."

While Harriet moved toward the platform, Kinsman turned and picked up a large box, beautifully wrapped and be-ribboned. As he stepped to the front of the stage to meet Harriet, he stumbled and dropped the box. It crashed to the floor with the horrible sound of shattering glass.

Turned out the box was filled with broken beer bottles, cracked window panes and other bits of glass. Crystal indeed! Wives bore no immunity from my zany cohorts.

16

Potpourri

Kids, red Indians and friendly lions

Dear Boeing—It's distressing to realize how many screwballs are at liberty in our society. And most of them, at one time or another, write letters to large companies—quite frequently to Boeing. Such letters wound up in public relations. Most were disposed of in File G—the round file. A few examples:

Dear Sir:

I might wind up in the nuthouse as a result of this letter. (I've been there three times.) But to hell with it, I'll take a chance. Try to find out if I do and if so, fourth time, slip me a mickey of whiskey when the bastards aren't looking.

C.W.

Dearest President:

The world will owe you a debt of gratitude if you started manufacturing heavy mining equipment. Some of your jets would be used to transport. May too the day come when you will produce electro-nuclear airplanes.

Harriet T.

✈ ✈ ✈

May I ask you good people. Are you in any way connected with Jehova's Witnesses that have organization all over the face of the earth. Or are you connected with the black serpent of confiscation with organizations on this central hemisphere riding the black sea of possession. The reason is that I am one of its victims. Awaiting your ans. I remain sincerely.

Private Citizen

✈ ✈ ✈

Mr. William Allen, President.

This is your phone number 656-2121. Right? Send all you can. Thank you.

S.D.C.

✈ ✈ ✈

Dear Sirs:

For 10 years I have been developing thoughts as to need of one complete tool organization, having their own mines and forest, their own manufacturing and research facilities. The purpose for your organization in this operation is investment. I would give a note and mortgage for 5 percent of the stock which I would pay for out of earnings as president. I would like the same arrangement with the 11 fellows I would like to have with me as directors. At school for graduation I was voted boy most likely to succeed. I feel I have.

✈ ✈ ✈

Mr. Boeing.

I am good looking widow. Five years now. Please send me name and address eligible bachelor. I make one a good wife.

L.K.

✈ ✈ ✈ ✈ ✈

Kids Are Smart—More refreshing were the letters we received from school children. Since the Wright brothers first flew, flying and airplanes have held special interest for children, from grade school through the teens.

To meet the requests of these younger people for pictures, the public relations department developed a packet depicting the principal Boeing aircraft, from the B-17 onward. Requests for the packets averaged 50 to 100 week after week.

Then at the end of World War II the stream of requests turned into a flood. Most of the increased requests were from children in Holland. Nearly all wrote that they had watched the "Forts" flying across their occupied country during the war to bomb enemy targets. Then, they added, the B-17s were the first to drop relief supplies to them at war's end.

A most intriguing aspect of the letters from Holland was the clear penmanship and the precise English grammar. A sharp contrast to the average letter from American students.

✈ ✈ ✈

Modest Young Lady—Harold Dunn, in the 1960s, taught school in Ballwin, Missouri. He supplied

Boeing Magazine with excerpts from the more interesting of the themes on aviation, turned in by his
grade school pupils. Samples follow:

"Charles Lindbergh was the first to fly to Paris.
He did it by the airplane method."

"The Wright brothers made their first flight in
1903. 1903 was really in the 20th century, but every-
body was behind time in those days."

"Latitude tells you where you are and longitude
tells you how long you can stay there."

"Drone is a spare name for people who can't say
pilotless airplane."

"The three main men on an airplane are the pilot,
navigator and percolator."

A really smart young man wrote, "When anybody
says plane what he is saying depends on whether he
is saying it to a pilot or a carpenter."

A modest young lady wrote, "I know what a
sextant is but I had rather not say."

"The North Star is, as a mattery fact, almost
straight north. This is quite a coincidence."

"So far, planes have only been able to fly in circles
of no more than 360 degrees. This could be the next big
break-through in air travel."

(What are you Boeing engineers doing about
solving that 360 degree problem?)

✈ ✈ ✈ ✈ ✈

Friendly Lion—Most flamboyant character of
the 1930s was Roscoe Turner, he of the red-lined cape
and pet lion. His forte was to fly between any two
given cities and thus establish a speed record for that
particular route.

In 1933 Turner teamed with Clyde Pangborn to
enter the London-to-Australia air race. As their ve-
hicle they selected a Boeing 247, standard passenger

transport. Turner came to Seattle to pick up the aircraft. He was met by Fred Collins, who discovered that Turner had his pet lion Gilmore with him.

The lion was put in the back seat of Collins' car, and the two men sat in the front. "I halted at a stop sign at a cross street on Fourth Avenue South," Collins related. "As we paused there for a moment, that goddamn lion reached over and started licking my neck. I was so startled that I let out the clutch and we damn near collided with another car. Ever feel a lion's tongue? (Few people have.) It's about as rough as a rasp. Patsy (Fred's wife) thought Roscoe and I had. been drinking when we arrived home with the lion in tow. Somehow we survived the evening."

Turner and Pangborn took third in the 10,000-mile race. Gilmore stayed home.

✈ ✈ ✈ ✈ ✈

Red Indian in the Cockpit—The figure coming forward in the aisle toward the plane's cockpit wore the full ceremonial regalia of a Yakima Indian chief. The plane, a Boeing 377 Stratocruiser, was on a one-stop delivery flight to London. It was the first of three purchased by British Overseas Airways Corporation. The crew, from cabin attendants to flight deck, was all British.

Passengers included Boeing representatives, BOAC officials and a certain number of invited guests, including John Gibson of Yakima, Washington, noted as the owner of a buffalo ranch and aficionado of Indian lore. He was the father-in-law of Cecil Gholson, aide to Wellwood Beall, Boeing senior vice president. Cec arranged that Gibson make the flight as far as New York, where a number of the Boeing people would disembark. I was to continue on to work with the BOAC public relations people in London.

I dozed off in the routine of the flight but was startled to full awakeness when the "Indian chieftain" brushed by on his way toward the cockpit. His regalia included fine buckskin shirt and trousers, moccasins and a feathered headdress which reached down his back, almost to his ankles.

Since it was not a scheduled flight, the cockpit door was open so that guests might watch flight procedures. With gleeful anticipation I watched as Gibson entered the control cabin. The captain, jacket on and buttoned, cap at proper angle, was the epitome of an Englishman at his formal best. Gibson stood behind the flight engineer and just to the rear of the captain.

The captain turned to say something to the engineer when he saw the pseudo Indian chief. Startled, he started to rise but was restrained by his seat belt. A look of quizzical astonishment swept his face. Visions of those American "red Indians" and their scalping proclivities must have flashed through his mind. Cec relieved the situation by going forward to introduce his father-in-law and explain the costume.

On arrival in New York, Gibson still wore his Indian outfit. He was the focus of more attention from the gathering press than the airplane, to the unhappiness of the New York BOAC press representative.

We boarded a bus for the trip into the city and an overnight stay before continuing on to London. The bus drew up at the Lexington Avenue side of the Waldorf. I took a strategic position on the sidewalk to watch developments. It is well known that New Yorkers are the most inquisitive in the world. If one person bends over to pick up something, a half dozen will stop to see what he is doing. As Gibson, still in full regalia, stepped onto the sidewalk, people stopped in astonishment. The crowd grew until it was with difficulty that we made our way to the escalator and up to the registration desk. Again I stood back to watch the action. A morning-coated clerk was busy at the registration desk when he looked up—and jumped back in astonishment.

"Ah, er, that is, did you want something, sir?"

Someone in the party whispered to Gibson, "Tell him you wantum tepee."

Cec broke in to explain the setup.

I was disappointed that Gibson was not going on to London. I would have delighted to take him into the Savoy or Claridge's or perhaps a stroll along Piccadilly where he would have been worthy attention competition for the Piccadilly pigeons who work that thoroughfare.

The next day I learned about the Norman white horses. I was in the cockpit when the captain pointed to a Wales hillside and asked if I had seen the white horses as he pointed ahead. I searched but could see no grazing equines. Suddenly I became aware of a large white silhouette of a horse, many times larger than normal, on a hillside slope. The captain explained that the figures were carved into the underlying chalk of the countryside by the Normans during their invasion of England. Their significance is unknown, he said.

✈ ✈ ✈ ✈ ✈

Office Shuffle—With reassignment of office space on the first floor of the Administration Building, Jim Prince as a company vice president naturally had first choice. He opted for the series of offices along the front of the building facing East Marginal Way. He took the corner office. Public relations got the other side of the building. I had the opposite corner from Prince.

The basement of the Ad building comprises a garage for the cars of executives and for company pool cars. Jim Luster was in charge of the basement, keeping the cars washed and polished and having them warmed up when their owners were ready to leave. Typical of Boeing's "no perks" policy, the car owners had to pay Jim for the extra service out of their own pockets.

Entrance to the garage was down a ramp which had an electric eye automatically opening the overhead door when a car drove through. This entrance was directly under Prince's office. Every time that heavy door clanged shut, all the furniture in Jim's office would jump. Thud, and articles on his desk would shudder. However, Jim never demanded exchange of offices, nor complained of the unnerving banging. But, I did see him wince on occasion when the big bang occurred.

✈ ✈ ✈ ✈ ✈

A Social Tip—An important contract had been won by the Aerospace division, and to mark the occasion, a victory party was arranged. Among the attendees was one of the newer secretaries, a naive young lady of limited experience. She drank several cocktails in rapid succession and promptly fell, stiff-legged and as rigid as a felled tree.

The next day a management conference was held. Someone suggested the requirement for a policy statement regarding drinking at parties. T Wilson proposed the first qualification should be that if people were going to drink, they should learn to bend their knees if they fell down.

✈ ✈ ✈ ✈ ✈

Where's Santa?—The hard-working Boeing sales crew, headed by Wellwood Beall, was holding a number of sessions with various officials of Lufthansa, German airline, in Cologne, Germany. Beall was on the rotund side. His white hair and trim mustache gave him a distinguished appearance.

Each evening the group, after a hard day's work, would make its way to a favorite bar, a short distance from the Excelsior Ernst, their hotel across the street from the Dom, Cologne's famed cathedral. After several days the group had become well known to the barmaids, among them Gretchen, a buxom lass with wheat-colored hair.

One evening, after waiting some time for Beall, who had been detained at the Lufthansa offices, the several sales representatives decided to go on ahead to their usual "happy hour" at the bar. As they entered, Gretchen exclaimed: "Ach, here comes Boeing again, but where is the nice little man who looks like Santa Claus?"

✈ ✈ ✈ ✈ ✈

Varied Recruits—Recruiting of employees, whether professional, hourly or office, is an ongoing and interesting phase of Boeing operations. In times of particular needs recruiters cover the entire country, backed up by local advertising. Of course, the reverse is true, with competing companies seeking recruits in Boeing areas of operation.

The anticipations and company views of some of the interviewees are varied and in some cases almost disturbing as to the naivete of the applicants. In interviewing candidates for the public relations operation, one of my major questions was "Why do you want to get into public relations?"

One just-out-of-college applicant replied, "Oh, I want to travel and I understand you people go all over the world. I want to meet important people, plan programs and get to work with top management." "Wait a minute," I said, "apparently you want my job, and I intend to be around for a while."

On the other hand, a strong desire to get into public relations at whatever level and a determination to do so marked a young reporter from the *Wenatchee Daily World.* An opening had come up in our department, and we spread the word through the journalism grapevine.

Not trusting to mail or phoned application, Jim Boynton dashed over from Wenatchee and literally camped on our doorsteps. After I had interviewed him in the morning, I told him we would make our decision after interviewing other applicants.

It seemed to me that Jim phoned practically on the hour through the day to inquire if he had the job. Finally to stop the phone calls, I said, "Come on back and sign up." Actually, Jim was by far the best of those interviewed and still plays an important role in the public relations organization.

In the routine of signing up and hiring of potential employees, a number of routine questions were asked, and each applicant was given a questionnaire to fill out. Among the questions to be answered in writing was "Do you have a physical disability which would prevent you performing normal duties?"

One feminine applicant filled in the "physical disability" space with "occasional bladder problem" and added a post note "but only after sex."

The recruiter took the questionnaire to his supervisor. "How should I handle this one?" he asked.

"Just mark it, 'No sex on company property.'"

✈ ✈ ✈ ✈ ✈

It Can't Happen—In cooperation with a good customer, Pan American Airways, we had taken the Stratocruiser to Los Angeles for a press demonstration flight. The Pan Am public relations people had lined up a full load of representatives from the media—press, radio, magazines and motion pictures.

We gathered the group at Mike Lyman's restaurant on the second floor of one of the terminal buildings. When Elliott Merrill, pilot, wheeled the Stratocruiser into position, the guests were onloaded. Since there was a full load, I stayed behind and went to the balcony outside Lyman's to watch the take-off.

Following standard procedure, Merrill stopped at the end of the runway to run up and test the engines. As I watched the procedure, the nose of the plane seemed to lift slightly from the ground. I decided the Los Angeles shimmering heat waves had caused the distortion. Then, there it was again. The nose went up tentatively, teetered, then full up, smacking the tail solidly on the concrete. Elliott reduced power, the nose came down, and he taxied slowly back to the loading area.

"What happened?" I shouted to Elliott through his open cockpit window. "I don't know; we've got to check the tail," he said. I got the Pan Am P.R. reps and said, "Get everyone up in Mike's bar and don't let anyone near a telephone while we check this thing out." I had visions of what could be highly negative publicity both for the airline and Boeing.

In the hope that Seattle might have some explanation, I got Lysle Wood, chief engineer, on the phone and asked him what could have caused the nose to go up and the tail hit the ground during engine run-up.

"That's impossible," he said. "It just couldn't happen."

"Okay, it can't happen, but I just saw it."

"Impossible."

Meantime, the flight crew had made inspection and found two or three of the circumferentials of the tail section slightly flattened. They also found the logical explanation for the incident. Some 1,500 pounds of towing and other equipment had been stowed in the lower aft cargo hold. The run-up spot Merrill had selected was on a slight down slope from nose to tail of the plane. When Elliott ran the propellers through reverse, that, in combination with the weight at the rear, lifted the nose.

"Only minor damage," Elliott reported. "We'll make a quick test hop to check cabin pressurization." Back on the ground all operations were reported normal. Guests were re-loaded and enjoyed an hour flight out over the Mojave Desert.

None of the media reported the minor contretemps, to the relief of Pan Am and Boeing representatives.

If I remember correctly, Lysle Wood did agree that, under the circumstances, it could happen.

✈ ✈ ✈ ✈ ✈

Wrong Way, Sister—Having two brothers, Al and Bob, who flew and owned their own airplanes, I decided it behooved me to at least learn to fly. I got through the instruction period, solo cross country and earned my private license.

Returning one day from a flight to Shelton, I reported to the Boeing Field control tower, "Over the north end of Vashon Island for landing Boeing Field." I was advised "Landing runway three-one (31) report over the reservoir." The majority of landings at Boeing Field are made on the one-three (13) runways because of the prevailing wind, that is, most landings are to the southeast; runway three-one is for landings to the northwest.

I left the radio tuned to the tower, and as I neared the reservoir, I heard an exasperated voice speaking slowly and distinctly, "Did you understand that I said runway three-one, repeat, three-one?"

A feminine voice came on the air, "Oh dear, I'm so used to landing in the other direction on one-three that I've got things all fouled up, haven't I?"

A couple of us got "go arounds" while the confused sister landed on the wrong runway.

✈ ✈ ✈ ✈ ✈

Just a Day at the Office—Sales conferences and demonstrations in Europe highly essential to program. Agreed. However, plane can be spared from test program for only three or four days.

Take off of the 707 with Tex Johnston at the controls was at 3 p.m. Seattle time. Rome our destination, with an estimated 13 hours flight time.

Just a few minutes out, over the north end of Lake Chelan, when, damn, a stuck fuel flow valve on one of the engines. Tex turned back. Over Puget Sound he dumped several thousand gallons of fuel to reduce the landing weight. A two-hour delay and we were off again.

The great circle route to Rome runs far north in Canada. As we passed over Hudson Bay, the sun was just setting in the west in colors ranging from bright red in the north to deep purple to the south. In the east the color effect was repeated as the sun was starting to rise. Very impressive. Farther north and the sun would not have set at all.

On time in Rome after a 13-hour six-minute flight. Enough fuel remained that we could have gone on to Cairo or Athens.

"Nice landing, Tex," I said.

"No. I dropped it about two inches."

✈ ✈ ✈ ✈ ✈

Schedule for the Next Day—Ken Luplow, Boeing European representative, had arranged conferences and demonstrations with five major airlines in five different countries! At the same time, similar meetings with the press of the several countries were to be held.

Eight o'clock and an early morning session at Rome airport. Then off to Paris. Sales and other company officials met with their counterparts from Air France. Raymond DeLobel and Sandrik Couris, our Paris public relations representatives, had the media on hand.

On to Brussels for sessions with Sabena and beer with the press. On the road again to Frankfort for a repeat performance with Lufthansa and schnapps and sausage with the media. Curtain down in London with BOAC meeting. More press. Sherry and biscuits.

Early the next morning the 707 took off for the return trip to Seattle. I am staying over in London but go to see the troops depart. We put aboard the plane early morning editions of London papers with which to surprise Seattle friends who will read them mid-morning of the same day.

Five countries, five press sessions, five serious discussions with prospective customers and back to the salt mines. The 707 missed only three days from the test program, and one of them was a no-count Sunday.

Just another day at the office!

✈ ✈ ✈ ✈ ✈

Why 707?—Boeing people are frequently asked how it happens that all Boeing commercial jet transports carry 700 numbers. Both order and logic are behind the system.

Shortly after the company was formed in 1916, a numbering system was established to cover all company products. Zero to 100 were assigned to various aircraft and airfoil sections as were 100 to 200. The 200 series was applied to airplane designs solely and included the famed B-17—company designation, the 299. The 300 series included the 307 Stratoliner, the 314 Clipper flying boats, the B-29 and B-50 bombers, and the twin-deck Stratocruiser series.

The 400 series covered bombers, including the B-47 and B-52. The 500 series was reserved for industrial products, and the 600 series for guided missile programs such as GAPA and BOMARC. (GAPA—Ground-to-Air Pilotless Aircraft; BOMARC—Boeing-Michigan Aeronautical Research Center.)

When the prototype 707 was being designed, it was disguised as a Stratocruiser derivative, carrying the engineering number 367-80 to hide the development from competitors. Hence the Dash-80 designation generally used.

As the design went into production, the 700 series was created. The sales department, under Wellwood Beall, proposed that the first jet passenger plane be named the Boeing 707 Jet Stratoliner and the long-range version be termed the Boeing 707 Jet Intercontinental Stratoliner. The first advertisements announcing the new planes came out with these names.

Public Relations argued that the prime objective was to associate Boeing with the jet age. Further, that the long designations were unwieldy, did not fit newspaper headlines or journalistic "lead" policies, and just wouldn't work. The company's advertising agency, the nationally known N.W. Ayer and Son, agreed with the stand. Public Relations also pointed out that the 700 numbering system could be projected into the future—the 727, 737, etc.—with a cumulative promotional effect. The argument prevailed, and the first model was identified simply as the "Boeing 707." The models have progressed through 727, 737, 747, 757 and 767. Who knows, perhaps beyond lie the 777, 787 and the 797.

✈ ✈ ✈ ✈ ✈

Crash Landing—I seem to have a propensity for gathering "firsts." First to cross the U.S. without visiting the restroom. First to hit a queen with a snowball. First to crash in a flight training session.

A Link trainer is a simulation of a plane cockpit, complete with all controls and instruments, but forever ground-bound. The controls and instruments react exactly as they would in a plane in flight. The "cabin" tilts and turns, tips up and down, all to simulate the movements of an airplane as the controls are actuated.

I had been in the Link for a half hour, had executed various maneuvers as directed, and now at 5,000 feet altitude was ordered to return to Boeing Field and land. I turned to the proper heading, set up a standard rate of descent, and advised the "tower" of my position and intention to land.

At 3,000 feet I was proceeding in normal fashion when suddenly the "cockpit" dropped sharply to the left, the instruments indicated a half-dozen different situations, and I cracked my head on the side of the cabin.

"Some joker has cranked in an impossible situation to test my reactions," was my first thought. Try as I might I couldn't get the "plane" back to wings level and normal descent.

"Jeeze, you've crashed!" I heard laughter from outside. "You aren't dead. Open up."

Back on floor level I learned that one of the actuating arms which tilts the simulator had broken, hence the violent reaction. Never had been known to happen before. So, I became the first to crash in a Link!

✈ ✈ ✈ ✈ ✈

Grandma's Cookies—Jon and Maureen Chilwell published a monthly aviation magazine *Wings Over Africa* in Johannesburg, South Africa. On a visit to Seattle and the Boeing Company, they were being entertained at Canlis, one of Seattle's outstanding restaurants, located on a hillside overlooking Lake Union.

As the group chatted over after-dinner coffee, Maureen suddenly burst into laughter.

"What's so amusing?" she was asked.

"Look! Advertised in neon lights. This is price-
less!" And she pointed across the lake to the
"Grandma's Cookies" sign atop a large bakery.

To her bewildered hosts she explained that in
South Africa a "cookie" is a street walker.

English may be a common language, but it be-
hooves one to be aware of local usage.

✈ ✈ ✈ ✈ ✈

38 MPG! Wow!—The DPC building and its annex were government-constructed buildings to house
various Air Force and other defense officials assigned
to Boeing. Since there was unused space in the buildings, Boeing was given permission to place certain
activities in the area.

A section of company accounting was transferred
to the new quarters. In this particular group was a
young man who in Elizabethan days would have been
termed a "dandy" or a "fop." Conscious of latest styles,
he had learned that derby hats were quite the "in"
thing, or "the cat's pajamas" as was the popular
phrase of that day. Mighty proud of his derby, his
name in gold on the inner band, he would polish it on
his sleeve and stand in front of a mirror to adjust it to
the right angle before venturing out.

This was too much for a group of his co-workers.
They got together and purchased two exact duplicate
derbies and had the chap's name embossed in each as
in the original. However, one of the hats was a size
smaller than his, the other a size larger. The next day
they slyly replaced his regular hat with the smaller of
the two they had bought. Our dandy went to the
mirror, tried to put his hat on, took it off and looked to
see if his name was in it. Tried it on again. Impossible

to know what went through his mind. Could a hat shrink? Nevertheless, he ventured out with the hat riding high on his locks. Later his regular hat was switched back, and he was allowed to proceed in peace for three or four days. Each time he put his hat on he would look at the inside to make sure his name was there.

Then the culprits struck again, substituting the over-size hat. When he carefully lowered the hat to his head, after the usual inspection check, it dropped down almost to his ears. Torture must have been his. Nevertheless he ventured forth, looking somewhat like a pushcart peddler from New York's Lower East Side.

The boys decided they had had their fun, restored the original hat, recovered the substitutes and set about dreaming up the next adventure.

Alas for the guileless lad, his torment was not over. A few months after the hat bit, the chap bought a new Volkswagen. It was one of the first in the Seattle area after their introduction in the U.S. following World War II. The new owner was particularly proud of his car's economy. "I'm getting 36 miles per gallon," he boasted. Bingo! Several of his co-workers again got their heads together.

They waited until the gas tank was about half empty, then refilled it to the top. "Gee, I got 45 miles per gallon," the lad declared. Another wait until the tank was almost empty, then another refill. "You won't believe this, but I'm getting 51 miles to the gallon. Guess it was just a matter of the engine getting broken in."

Now into reverse. Gas was siphoned from the tank. Mileage dropped to 26 and even down to 19 miles to the gallon. The bug owner was beside himself.

"Those Germans aren't so hot as car builders," he observed of the craftsmen he had been praising only a short time before.

The pranksters decided to cease their nefarious activity. As his mileage went back to normal, the lad gave praise to his dealer, who had "located a problem built into the machine by the Germans."

✈ ✈ ✈ ✈ ✈

It's a Small World—Cliches are only cliches because over time they have proved to be true. Thus "It's a small world" has real meaning to me.

On vacation in Zermatt, Switzerland, at the foot of the Matterhorn (public relations people do get a week or two vacation every eight or 10 years), I got to talking to Elsie, the barmaid at the Monte Cervin Hotel. In the course of a general conversation, she asked where I lived.

"Well, Elsie, it's a bit hard to explain. I live way up in the far corner of the United States, almost to Alaska, in a city called Seattle."

"Seattle! King Street Station," she exclaimed. Seems that on a North American tour the year before she had had to lay over between trains for three hours in the King Street Station. Did she know Seattle!

Because I had heard so much about the exclusive digs of sheiks, kings and the multi-rich, I summoned enough nerve to enter the portals of Claridge's in London. Trying to look important, I sat in the lobby observing the clientele.

Suddenly in walked Harry O'Connor, of N.W. Ayer and Son, our advertising agency. First time I had seen him away from the Philadelphia offices. Heading for a nearby restaurant, we took a shortcut through

Shepherds Court, stopping to read some of its offers of massage and other benefits to be had from caring young ladies.

Another time. Rome and the Via Venato. I was walking from the Excelsior to the American embassy when I saw a familiar figure—Glen Dierst, at that time head of plant protection at company headquarters. He was on a rare vacation from official duties.

This time it was Sydney, Australia. Escorted to a table in the upstairs dining room of Cunningham's in Kings Cross, I was hailed from a nearby table. Beckoning me was Ben Werner, Boeing engineer and mayor of Mercer Island, whose home was only about a mile from mine.

And again it was Cologne, Germany, and the Excelsior Ernst Hotel. Strolling through the lobby and trying to resist the temptation to enter the attractive bar, I heard my name called from within its portals. Bob Kinkaid, Jim Murray's right-hand man in the Boeing Washington office, and Art Curran, Boeing test pilot, made the excellent suggestion that I join them.

Johannesburg, South Africa. I stopped in a shop to purchase a finger piano and two native-carved masks to which I had taken a fancy. Arrangements were being made to have the articles shipped home. When I gave a Seattle address, the sales lady exclaimed, "Seattle! I have a cousin there. She lives on Snokelme Street. Maybe you know her." Took a bit of sorting out to decipher that the lady was referring to Snoqualmie Street. No, I didn't know her cousin.

Index